T0360616

Higher Education and Policy for Creative Economies in Africa

The book reflects on the role of the creative economies in a range of African countries (namely Ghana, Kenya, Nigeria, South Africa and Uganda). Chapters explore how creative economies emerge and can be supported in African countries.

The contributors focus on two key dimensions: the role of higher education and the role of policy. Firstly, they consider the role of higher education and alternative forms of specialised education to reflect on how the creative aspirations of students (and future creative workers) of these countries are met and developed. Secondly, they explore the role of policy in supporting the agendas of the creative economy, taking also into consideration the potential historical dimension of policy interventions and the impact of a lack of policy frameworks. The book concludes by reflecting on how these two pillars of creative economy development, which are usually taken for granted in studying creative economies in the Global North, need to be understood with their own specificity in the context of our selected case studies in Africa.

This book will be of interest to students, scholars and professionals researching the creative economies in Africa across the humanities and social sciences.

Roberta Comunian is Reader in Creative Economy at the Department for Culture, Media and Creative Industries at King's College London, UK.

Brian J. Hracs is an Associate Professor of Human Geography at the University of Southampton, UK.

Lauren England is Baxter Fellow in Creative Economies at Duncan of Jordanstone College of Art & Design at the University of Dundee, UK.

Routledge Contemporary Africa Series

Health and Care in Old Age in Africa
Edited by Pranitha Maharaj

Rethinking African Agriculture
How Non-Agrarian Factors Shape Peasant Livelihoods
Edited by Goran Hyden, Kazuhiko Sugimura and Tadasu Tsuruta

Toward an Animist Reading of Postcolonial Trauma Literature
Reading Beyond the Single Subject
Jay Rajiva

Development-induced Displacement and Human Rights in Africa
The Kampala Convention
Romola Adeola

Death and the Textile Industry in Nigeria
Elisha P. Renne

Modern Representations of Sub-Saharan Africa
Edited by Lori Maguire, Susan Ball and Sébastien Lefait

Narrating Human Rights in Africa
Eleni Coundouriotis

Higher Education and Policy for Creative Economies in Africa
Developing Creative Economies
Edited by Roberta Comunian, Brian J. Hracs and Lauren England

For more information about this series, please visit: https://www.rou
tledge.com/Routledge-Contemporary-Africa/book-series/RCAFR.

Higher Education and Policy for Creative Economies in Africa

Developing Creative Economies

Edited by

Roberta Comunian, Brian J. Hracs and Lauren England

Routledge
Taylor & Francis Group

LONDON AND NEW YORK

First published 2021
by Routledge
2 Park Square, Milton Park, Abingdon, Oxon OX14 4RN

and by Routledge
52 Vanderbilt Avenue, New York, NY 10017

Routledge is an imprint of the Taylor & Francis Group, an informa business

British Library Cataloguing-in-Publication Data
A catalogue record for this book is available from the British Library

Library of Congress Cataloging-in-Publication Data
Names: Comunian, Roberta, editor. | Hracs, Brian J., editor. |
England, Lauren, editor.
Title: Higher education and policy for creative economies in Africa:
developing creative economies/edited by Roberta Comunian,
Brian J. Hracs and Lauren England.
Other titles: Routledge contemporary Africa series.
Description: Abingdon, Oxon; New York, NY: Routledge, 2021. |
Series: Routledge contemporary Africa | Includes bibliographical
references and index. | Identifiers: LCCN 2020036983 (print) |
LCCN 2020036984 (ebook) | ISBN 9780367481957 (hardback) |
ISBN 9781003127802 (ebook)
Subjects: LCSH: Cultural industries–Africa. | Cultural industries–
Government policy–Africa. | Arts–Study and teaching (Higher)–Africa.
| Economic development–Effect of education on–Africa.
Classification: LCC HD9999.C9473 A3553 2021 (print) |
LCC HD9999.C9473 (ebook) | DDC 338.477096–dc23
LC record available at https://lccn.loc.gov/2020036983
LC ebook record available at https://lccn.loc.gov/2020036984

ISBN: 978-0-367-48195-7 (hbk)
ISBN: 978-1-003-12780-2 (ebk)

Typeset in Bembo
by Deanta Global Publishing Services, Chennai, India

We would like to dedicate this book to all the research participants, creative practitioners and academic colleagues we have met during our fieldwork in Kenya, Nigeria and South Africa, as without their support and engagement this book would not have become a reality.

RC, BJH and LE

Contents

Figures

Tables

Contributors

Dr Oluwayemisi Adebola Abisuga-Oyekunle is a Post-Doctoral Research Fellow at the Department of Industrial Engineering, Tshwane University of Technology (South Africa). Her research interests include arts, cultural and creative industries, cultural policy, Indigenous Knowledge Systems, and SMEs. She is currently involved in the CatChain project, an EU-Horizon 2020 research initiative on global value chains. She is also involved in community development projects in Africa, on training and empowerment of youths and women in the production of handicraft products.

Madinatu Bello attended the University of Cape Coast and the University of Ghana for her first and second degrees respectively. Since 2013, she has been teaching at the University of Cape Coast (Ghana) as an Assistant Lecturer in the Department of Theatre and Film Studies. She is currently pursuing her PhD in an area of personal and professional interest, researching the cultural and creative industries and their connections with performing arts departments in universities in Ghana.

Dr Roberta Comunian is Reader in Creative Economy at the Department for Culture, Media and Creative Industries at King's College London (UK). She is interested in the cultural policy, cultural and creative work and creative higher education. She has published extensively on the role of creative and cultural industries in local development. She has coordinated two Arts and Humanities Research Council (AHRC) international research networks and is currently involved in the H2020 EU funded project DISCE: Developing inclusive and sustainable creative economies.

Fiona Drummond obtained her bachelors, honours and masters with distinction, majoring in geography and economics from Rhodes University (South Africa). Her master's thesis on cultural and creative industries cluster mapping and its link to socio-economic development in rural areas won the Economics Society of South Africa's Founder's Prize for the best masters by research in the country. Her research interests also include cultural and creative tourism and festivals.

James Drummond is Senior Lecturer in the Department of Geography of the North West University (South Africa), where he has taught for over 30 years. He has degrees from the University of Glasgow in Scotland and Witwatersrand in South Africa. He has published on rural and agricultural development in South Africa. His current interests lie in small town development and the cultural and creative economy.

Dr Lauren England is Baxter Fellow in Creative Economies at Duncan of Jordanstone College of Art & Design at the University of Dundee (UK). Her PhD at King's College London in partnership with Crafts Council UK investigated higher education and business development in UK contemporary craft. Lauren has published research on craft skills evolution, higher education and social enterprises. Her current research explores sustainable creative economy development in both Global North and Global South contexts.

Dr Brian J. Hracs is Associate Professor of Human Geography in the School of Geography and Environmental Science at the University of Southampton (UK). He is interested in how digital technologies and global competition are reshaping the marketplace for cultural products and the working lives and spatial dynamics of entrepreneurs and intermediaries in the creative economy. Brian has published articles about the music and fashion industries, value creation and the mobilities of 'talent'. He is currently researching the processes and spatial dynamics of curation, the trans-local nature of cultural scenes and creative economies in Africa.

Dr Shaibu Hassan Husseini is a Teaching Fellow at the Department of Mass Communication of the University of Lagos (Nigeria). He has considerable industry experience in Culture and Film Journalism, Broadcasting, Film Production Management and in Public Relations and Advertising. His current research interest is in the evaluation of the power structure and economics of motion picture production in Nigeria.

Victoria Isabelle Kay is an inspirational and well-connected business advisor, mentor and researcher. With a deep knowledge of fundraising and networking mechanisms, Victoria has extensive international experience in value adding and strategic partnership building at macro (policy) and micro (projects) levels. Victoria collaborates closely with HATCH on strategy, global partnerships and research projects.

Gershom Kimera is a Film & TV Media Professional who recently completed his MSc studies in Film & TV Production at the University of Portsmouth (UK) with a dissertation researching Film & TV Creative Skills and Skill Gap in the Ugandan Film & TV media production industry published on https://www.ugandafilmskill.com. His interests are research in Culture & Creative Skills in Film and TV media industries, especially in higher education.

Yemisi Mokuolu is an independent producer and CEO of HATCH, which she founded in 2002 to support people in developing cultural change and social impact businesses, projects and ideas. Yemisi is best known for her work supporting the development of the creative industries across Africa and African creative content globally. She has worked with a wide range of industry stakeholders including the British Council, Goethe Institute, Institut Français and Old Mutual, delivering research, capacity building and knowledge transfer programmes.

Ogake Mosomi is a Tutorial Fellow at the School of the Arts and Design, University of Nairobi (Kenya). Her interests include developing practical training approaches for fashion designers and strengthening linkages between industry and academia. She is currently a Business Coach for the Fashion DNA Project run by the British Council, a program helping upcoming designers improve their businesses. Ogake is also a practising fashion designer specialising in creating high-end, bespoke bridal gowns.

Vincent Obia is a PhD candidate of Media and Culture at the Birmingham School of Media, Birmingham City University (UK). He is also an academic at the University of Lagos (Nigeria) and his research interests include new media governance and the creative industries.

Professor Duro Oni is of the Department of Creative Arts, University of Lagos (Nigeria) and a Fellow of the Nigerian Academy of Letters. His research interests are in the areas of Theatre Arts Design and Aesthetics, Cultural Studies and the Nigerian Film Industry. He has been a collaborator on the Understanding and Supporting Creative Economies in Africa project. He was also a member of the team on Nigerian Video/DVD Industry and the UK African Diaspora of the Ferguson Centre (UK). He recently co-edited *The Soyinka Impulse: Essays on Wole Soyinka* (2019).

Dr Cornelius Onyekaba is a Theatre and Film Studies Scholar and a Faculty member of the Department of Creative Arts, University of Lagos (Nigeria). He is a member of the College of Screeners of the African Movie Academy Awards (AMAA), the Black Star International Film Festival and Network of Festival Managers in West Africa under the auspices of the British Council. He is the curator of the Unilag-Africaribbean Carnival.

Claudia María Velilla-Zuloaga is an alumna of King's College London (UK), where she obtained an MA in Conflict, Security and Development. She is interested in several development sectors, especially education, gender and inclusion across different regions of the African continent. Claudia collaborates with HATCH as a researcher. She is currently working at Innovations for Poverty Action (IPA) on the Ivory Coast supporting project and policy development activities.

Foreword

By 'Funmi Olonisakin

Africa is changing profoundly. The cumulative influence of a growing pool of talented and entrepreneurial next generation Africans is producing an emergent creative economy, with the potential to fuel Africa's economic growth and human development. The notable success of Nollywood, for example, has brought African film and television to the fore of international attention, further reinforcing the potential for culture and creativity to produce income and promote development across the African continent. However, translating this potential into real and sustainable human development requires focused policy interventions as well as systematic linkage between knowledge institutions and a thriving creative sector. It is this, which makes this book timely and relevant.

Higher Education and Policy for Creative Economies in Africa shines a light on the dynamic intersections between Africa's cultural and creative community, policy development and higher education institutions. It underscores the vital importance of the connection between the university, industry and the policy community. Producing knowledge and developing the skills that will grow and sustain the creative sector is a prerequisite for managing this area of rapid change. Several of the chapters in this book point to the evolving relationship between higher education and a changing society that is characterised by the agency of creative and entrepreneurial Africans who serve as the engine room of that change. Capturing and reproducing this agency, much of which remains a feature of the informal economy in many parts of Africa, will require a process of institutionalisation both within higher education as well as in policy institutions.

This book highlights several layers of collaboration, which are significant for this emergent creative economy in Africa. The first is interdisciplinary collaboration that connects academics, practitioners and the policy community. The second is the systematic linkage between higher education and creative economies. In their conclusion to this book, the editors see higher education as an important "intermediary operating across creative economies, youth, policy and local development". Higher education institutions are invaluable for knowledge production and skills development. In addition to facilitating access to education for many talented young Africans, they can influence policy for the advancement of creative economies. Third and last is international collaboration at two levels – within and outside Africa – which is essential to the effort to strengthen Africa's creative economies. An expanding network of actors and intermediaries across Africa and meaningful collaboration between African and non-African actors and institutions are key features. This book is clearly an example of the latter. International collaboration between African and non-African higher education institutions on the one hand, and between higher education and national and global policy actors on the other, will be crucial drivers of progress if the emerging creative economies are to be consolidated and sustained.

The editors of this book rightly acknowledge that it is impossible to cover the subject of Africa's creative economies comprehensively in the space of one book. However, by focusing on the African countries that were researched for this book – Ghana, Kenya, Nigeria and Uganda – they are able to reflect on some of the emerging trends while providing valuable insights into the work of creative and cultural practitioners and the larger policy context in which they operate.

Finally, it is worth noting that the editors of this book, Roberta Comunian, Brian Hracs and Lauren England, have demonstrated an important practice in international collaboration, which is worthy of emulation. By working with researchers and authors from some of the African countries discussed in this book and co-authoring chapters with them, the voices of key African interlocutors on the subject of Africa's creative economies are projected. We need more of such collaborations between non-African and African academics and practitioners alike so as to give visibility to the evolutions occurring in Africa and to do so with integrity. I congratulate the three editors for bringing such a distinctive project to fine conclusion.

'Funmi Olonisakin
Professor of Security, Leadership and
Development and Vice-President and
Vice-Principal King's College London

Acknowledgements

First of all, we are very grateful for the financial support provided by the Arts and Humanities Research Council (AHRC, grant number AH/P005950/1) through the Global Challenges Research Fund (GCRF). The funding allowed the authors to conduct fieldwork in three African countries and establish a supportive research network across these countries and the UK.

We would like to thank our very supportive African colleagues who facilitated our fieldwork activities, contributed to the book or simply welcomed us and shared their views on creative economies in Africa. We acknowledge here their invaluable support in each of the countries we visited. We give special thanks to the following colleagues:

In Kenya, Ogake Mosomi and Professor Lilac Adhiambo Osanjo at the University of Nairobi and Wakiuru Njuguna at HEVA for guiding us during our visit to Nairobi and supporting our fieldwork activities.

In Nigeria, Professor Duro Oni and all the staff at the Creative Arts Department at the University of Lagos, Polly Alakija, Chairman of the Lagos State Council for Arts and Culture, and Ojoma Ochai at British Council Nigeria for introductions and valuable support in connecting with the local creative economies.

In South Africa, Professor Jen Snowball from Rhodes University, Unathi Lutshaba and staff of the South African Cultural Observatory (SACO) and Dr Irma Booyens and her colleagues at the Human Sciences Research Council.

We are also grateful to all the research participants who completed surveys, met us for interviews and attended our workshops. Their generosity and warmth have made our research journey not only interesting but also fulfilling. As a small token of thanks for all the support and help we have received from colleagues and co-authors in Africa, as editors we have decided to direct all the royalties from the publication of this book towards the work of The Craft and Design Institute (CDI) in South Africa. The CDI is a not for profit organisation working across South Africa supporting the development of sustainable craft and design businesses. The book royalties will specifically support their activities in capacity building for young creative practitioners from disadvantaged backgrounds.

For other valuable research exchanges during the project activities we also thank Taylor Brydges, Ayeta Anne Wangusa, Damilola Adegoke and Charlotte Campbell.

We are thankful also to the network project advisory board for their support, in particular, John Davies (NESTA), Yemisi Mokuolu (HATCH Ideas/ HATCH Africa), Dr Eka Ikpe (Africa Leadership Centre, King's College London), Genevieve Pace (British Council), Morag Shiach (Queen Mary University of London), Dr Caspar Melville (SOAS, University of London) and Yudhishthir Raj Isar.

Finally, each of the authors would like to thank their families.

Dr Comunian would like to thank especially Leonardo, nonna Giuseppina and nonno Italo for the amazing patience and support shown during the recent lockdown period, while she spent too much time on her laptop and too little time playing. This book is also the result of all their love and care.

Dr England gives special thanks to her parents, Rob and Gill England, for encouraging her to join the project, and for all the cups of tea that fuelled the final stages. Also, to her co-editors, Roberta and Brian, for inviting her on the journey.

Dr Hracs would like to thank Andrea and Henry for encouraging his engagement with the project and being understanding during my time away from home.

Abbreviations and acronyms

AGOA	African Growth and Opportunity Act
AFAC	African Arts and Craft Expo
AHRC	Arts & Humanities Research Council (UK)
ANC	African National Congress
ARUA	African Research Universities Alliance
BMAS	Benchmark Minimum Academic Standard (Nigeria)
CCIs	Cultural and Creative Industries
CCP	Creative and cultural policy
CDI	The Craft and Design Institute (South Africa)
CE	Creative Economy / Creative Economies
CIGS	Cultural Industries Growth Strategy (South Africa)
CNC	Centre for National Culture (Ghana)
CRA	Commission of Revenue Allocation (Kenya)
DAC	Department of Arts and Culture (South Africa)
DACST	Department of Arts, Culture, Science and Technology (South Africa)
DCMS	Department of Culture, Media and Sport (UK)
DIT	Directorate of Industrial Training (Kenya)
EPZ	Export Processing Zone
FGD	Focus Group Discussion
GCRF	Global Challenges Research Fund
GDP	Gross Domestic Product
HE	Higher education
HEIs	Higher education institutions
ILO	International Labour Organisation
ITC	International Trade Centre
K-U	Kinna-Uganda (Uganda)
MOPICON	Motion Picture Council of Nigeria (Nigeria)
MoU	Memorandum of Understanding

NAFEST	National Festival of Arts and Culture (Nigeria)
NCAC	National Council for Arts and Culture (Nigeria)
NEF	National Empowerment Fund (South Africa)
NPE	National Policy on Education (Nigeria)
NRF	National Research Fund (South Africa)
NUC	National Universities Commission (Nigeria)
ODA	Official Development Assistance
SABC	South African Broadcasting Corporation (South Africa)
SACO	South Africa Cultural Observatory (South Africa)
SBC	Small Business Centre (Kenya)
SCAC	State Council for Arts and Culture (Nigeria)
SEFA	Small Enterprise Finance Agency (South Africa)
SIWES	Student Industrial Work Experience Scheme (Nigeria)
STEAM	Science, Technology, Engineering, Art and Mathematics
TIVET	Technical Industrial Vocational and Entrepreneurship Training (Kenya)
UCC	University of Cape Coast (Ghana)
UCC	Uganda Communications Commission (Uganda)
UFF	Uganda Film Festival (Uganda)
UFN	Uganda Film Network (Uganda)
UG	Undergraduate
UNCTAD	United Nations Conference on Trade and Development
UNDP	United Nations Development Programme
UNESCO	United Nations Educational, Scientific and Cultural Organisation
VAC	Visual Arts and Craft
VEI	Vocational enterprise institutions (Nigeria)
VJ	Vee-Jay or Video Jockey

1 Introduction

Roberta Comunian, Brian J. Hracs and
Lauren England

The research journey behind the book

This book is the first of two edited collections that have emerged as a result of an Arts & Humanities Research Council (AHRC) funded international research network connected to the Global Challenges Research Fund (GCRF) entitled "Understanding and Supporting Creative Economies in Africa: Education, Networks and Policy". The funding scheme and the network that was established throughout its development (2018–2020) have allowed the authors to not only engage with the current research, knowledge, and practices of African creative economies but also to collect data first-hand about their development and trajectory.

In approaching this research, we have tried to adopt an inclusive perspective and definition of creative economies, beginning by mapping current knowledge and approaches but also considering how the newly established network could contribute to a better understanding of the sector. We nevertheless remain aware of its limitations, particularly regarding the geographical scope of the book as well as the methodological perspective adopted.

Researching in Africa and writing about Africa

Throughout the project we have been conscious of the claim of researching creative economies *in Africa*. The size of Africa and the impossibility for our chapter selection to represent all its diversity of contexts, histories and conditions is a clear challenge for the research and this edited book. Our research network limited its activities to three African countries, where fieldwork was undertaken in 2019: Nigeria (April 2019), South Africa (June 2019) and Kenya (September 2019). Even within this limited number of countries our claims and research only really stretch as far as one of their principal cities, respectively Lagos, Cape Town and Nairobi. However, within this book there are contributions from a few more countries, including Ghana (Chapter 3), Uganda (Chapter 5) and a more general overview of the African context (Chapter 8). This has been the result of colleagues' work, engaging with the project in international events and exchanges, in addition to countries where we were able to conduct research. While the contribution can only represent a few African countries and case studies, we believe the value of the themes and approaches discussed can not only have an impact across many other African countries but also provide broader lessons beyond the African continent.

Researching complex creative economies

Having previously studied creative economies extensively (but not in the context of Africa), we were very aware that studying creative work and creative industries requires a complex understanding of a range of factors and forces across a variety of scales (Comunian, 2019). At the micro-scale, we had previously looked extensively at dynamics of work (Comunian, 2009; Hauge and Hracs, 2010) and learning practices (England, 2020), as well as markets (Hracs et al., 2013) for creative individuals. By extension we were also very aware of the role of place (Brydges and Hracs, 2019), cities and regions as well as policy frameworks (Chapain and Comunian, 2010) that might support or hinder the development of creative economies. However, given the limitations on time (a two-year project) and resources, the best approach was for us to focus on the meso-level and the role of networks and intermediaries (Comunian, 2010; Hracs, 2015) in creative economies. While this remains a partial perspective on the whole system, it nevertheless gave insights into the activities of creative and cultural practitioners (micro-level) and the high-level policy frameworks in which these intermediaries operated (macro-level). This provided a bird's-eye view on the creative economies from the perspective of different organisations and individuals that work towards supporting and developing it.

With the specific framework provided by these two considerations, four key themes emerged in our research and exchanges with colleagues and researchers in Africa. The four themes are addressed across two edited books. In this first book, we consider the role of higher education and policy for the development of creative economies in Africa; in the second (forthcoming) edited book we will explore creative work and co-working alongside clustering and networking dynamics in African creative economies. In this book, our reflections on higher education and policy are highly connected with the work of a range of intermediaries engaging in skills provision and education as well as wider support.

Defining creative economies: inclusivity and sustainability

In order to understand the chapters included in this book and the contribution they make it is vital to define what we mean by *creative economies*. It is crucial to clarify how this term connects with other terms used in the literature and by different authors in this book, namely creative and cultural industries (CCIs), creative economy (CE) and creative and cultural policy (CCP).

Since the 1998 Department for Digital, Culture, Media & Sport (DCMS) Mapping Document attempted to define the creative industries in the UK much attention has been paid to trying to measure and define the sector internationally. The section on creative industries (DCMS, 1998) has however been considered a very narrow model to adopt internationally and has been widely criticised for its commercial focus, strongly connected to its need to emphasise economic contributions. The creative industries definition clashed and overlapped with the previous terminology (namely cultural industries) which instead placed more emphasis on the fields of cultural productions included. The use of the term creative and cultural industries in the book acknowledges this broader and more encompassing understanding.

The work of the United Nations Conference on Trade and Development (UNCTAD and UNDP, 2010) positions the creative economy more strongly in an international framework. They see it as an evolving concept connected with the potential of creative activities and goods to generate economic impact and development. The United Nations Educational, Scientific and Cultural Organisation (UNESCO)'s framework for cultural statistics (UNDP and UNESCO, 2013) also recognises this as an ecosystem of activities, connected to cultural domains and CCIs but expanding to more sectors of society (for example, education and preservation) and relating both to intangible and tangible culture. In this respect, within this book, we want to build on the view presented by UNDP and UNESCO (2013: 12) that the "creative economy is not a single superhighway, but a multitude of different local trajectories found in cities and regions in developing countries". We push this argument further by suggesting that it is crucial to acknowledge that there is not one single creative economy but a multiplicity of creative economies which can feature overlapping and diverging agendas. This accounts for the range of business models and objectives which often extend to the social sphere (Comunian et al., 2020) as well as for new accounts of the connection between creativity and cultural development (De Beukelaer, 2015; Wilson et al., 2020). In our work, while we recognise the value of univocal definitions for collecting and comparing statistical data, conducting qualitative work and reflecting on the work of intermediaries or policy initiatives with an open and inclusive approach allowed us to capture a range of dynamics and experiences.

About this book

The book contains eight contributions from a multidisciplinary network involving both academic researchers and practitioners engaged in research across the African continent. While the case studies and reflections presented are limited and cannot represent the whole of Africa, they offer insights which we feel are of value beyond their geographical base and nature. They provide a critical platform to consider both the role of higher education and policy in a dialogical way, connecting theories to African-specific practices, approaches and challenges. The book is structured in two parts. The first considers the role played by higher education (HE) and the second focuses on the role played by policy.

Higher education and creative economies development

The first part of the book includes four papers that reflect on the role of HE in the development of creative economies in four African countries: Nigeria, Ghana, Kenya and Uganda. Beyond highlighting some of the specificities of those countries, these chapters also address a range of creative disciplines and fields, from the creative arts and theatre studies to fashion, film and television studies.

In the second chapter, **Obia et al.** reflect on the existing links between HE and the creative economy in Nigeria, using the case study of the Department of Creative Arts at the University of Lagos. It examines the support that the university provides for the creative economy in shaping and developing the talent needed in the sector, and the opportunities it makes available for creative students. Using a focus group comprising 15 educators, the chapter shows that the university provides a vital link between students and the creative economy. However, the chapter also reveals the challenges connected with the societal perception that creative studies do not lead to viable careers.

In the third chapter, **Bello** explores the context of collaborations between academia and the CCIs in Ghana. She begins by providing an overview of the HE framework for collaborations and curriculum development in Ghana. Afterwards, she looks more closely at the case study of the Theatre Studies department at the University of Cape Coast. Using a qualitative approach, she highlights how collaborations are perceived as informal, mostly of individual initiative rather than departmental, quite hierarchical and of short-term nature. Despite the positive impact on academics and students, she argues there is a need for more formal frameworks for collaborations to create real impact within and outside of HE.

In the fourth chapter, **England et al.** focus on HE provision in Kenya in relation to fashion design. They use data collected from Nairobi-based fashion designers to reflect on the training they undertook and their professional development, addressing the challenges faced by fashion design HE in trying to bridge practical and academic knowledge for the development of the sector. It also considers the value that investment in this area of work could have for the development of local supply chains that value original fashion production in Kenya instead of focusing on the simple manufacturing of garments in the country which does not develop local skills.

In the fifth chapter, **Comunian and Kimera** present the landscape of skills and HE provision in Uganda in relation to the film and television sector. They demonstrate that film and television in Africa have recently received a lot of attention, due to the international success of Nollywood. However, the reality of film production knowledge and skills is very different across African countries, and there are limited reliable data in most cases. One such context that has struggled to emerge internationally has been Uganda. The Ugandan film and television sector (Kinna-Uganda) is discussed in relation to the possibility for training and professional development, from HE to industry. Finally, structural conditions are considered as well as opportunities for international collaboration that might facilitate the international recognition of Kinna-Uganda talent.

The role of policy for creative economies

In the second part of the book, we focus on the role of policy in the development of creative economies. In this section two chapters remind us of the importance of looking at creative and cultural policy from a historical and longitudinal perspective. This allows us to discuss how changes over time affect the sector but also how policy focus and perspective themselves are often time-bound or influenced by broader political and infrastructural changes. The other two chapters offer a contemporary take, one reflecting on finance for CCIs and another looking at the role of policy in a specific sector, craft.

In the sixth chapter, **Oni et al.** offer a longitudinal perspective on cultural policy development in Nigeria. They chronicle the establishment of the State Councils for Arts and Culture (SCAC) and the

National Council for Arts and Culture (NCAC). The chapter reflects on the role of state and national cultural institutions, which have had a chequered history of performance and survival ranging from merely existing to making noticeable impacts on Nigerian cultural policy. In particular, they look at the importance of NAFEST, the National Festival of Arts and Culture, and the evolution of its changing theme and focus over time as an opportunity to discuss how culture is connected to Nigeria's development. They conclude by arguing for the importance of funding to enable a more structural engagement of cultural policy with local economic and cultural development.

In the seventh chapter, **Drummond and Drummond** look at the case of Mahikeng in South Africa and reflect on how it constituted an example of a policy-implemented creative and cultural cluster in the 1980s even before attention towards the clustering of CCIs was high on the academic and policy agenda. However, Mahikeng's cluster developed as a state-led initiative and declined when support and funding diminished. In the case of Mahikeng, even with the development of the Mahika-Mahikeng Festival, there was not a full return to its former glory. The authors reflect on the importance of hybrid forms of cluster development and management and the importance of private as well as community involvement.

In the eighth chapter, **Mokuolu et al.** consider the issue of finance for the development of CCIs across Africa. They reflect on when and how finance is needed in the development of creative ideas and creative business and highlight the importance of understanding finance for CCIs as an ecosystem. Drawing on qualitative interviews from across a range of sectors and stakeholders, the authors map needs and challenges that CCIs encountered when requiring finance and business support on the continent of Africa. They conclude that despite a great potential for growth, the landscape for CCIs in Africa is still limited and fragmented.

In the final chapter, **Abisuga-Oyekunle et al.** reflect on the role of policy in South Africa with reference to a specific sector, handicraft. They review the current knowledge and understanding of craft and its role in local development in the case of rural South Africa. Using qualitative interviews with small rural craft businesses, including makers, makers and retailers and only retailers, they explore the revenues and motivations of the businesses. They consider what forms of support the craft businesses accessed and what needs they expressed. The chapter concludes by arguing for a systematic understanding of the role that policy can play in supporting the craft sector, across social, economic, cultural and educational policy actions.

References

Brydges T and Hracs BJ (2019) The locational choices and interregional mobilities of creative entrepreneurs within Canada's fashion system. *Regional Studies* 53(4): 517–527.

Chapain CA and Comunian R (2010) Enabling and inhibiting the creative economy: The role of the local and regional dimensions in England. *Regional Studies* 43(6): 717–734.

Comunian R (2009) Questioning creative work as driver of economic development: The case of Newcastle-Gateshead. *Creative Industries Journal* 2(1): 57–71.

Comunian R (2010) Rethinking the creative city: The role of complexity, networks and interactions in the urban creative economy. *Urban Studies* 48(6): 1157–1179.

Comunian R (2019) Complexity thinking as a coordinating theoretical framework for creative industries research. In: Cunningham S and Flew T (eds) *A research agenda for creative industries*. Edward Elgar, Cheltenham, 39–57.

Comunian R, Rickmers D and Nanetti A (2020) Guest editorial: The creative economy is dead – Long live the creative-social economies. *Social Enterprise Journal* 16(2): 101–119.

DCMS (1998) *Creative industries mapping document*. DCMS, London. Available at: https://www.gov.uk/government/publications/creative-industries-mapping-documents-1998.

De Beukelaer C (2015) *Developing cultural industries: Learning from the palimpsest of practice*. European Cultural Foundation, Amsterdam.

England L (2020) *Crafting professionals in UK higher education: Craft work logics and skills for professional practice*. (unpublished doctoral thesis) King's College London, London.

Hauge A and Hracs BJ (2010) See the sound, hear the style: Collaborative linkages between Indie musicians and fashion designers in local scenes. *Industry and Innovation* 17: 113–129.

Hracs BJ (2015) Cultural intermediaries in the digital age: The case of independent musicians and managers in Toronto. *Regional Studies* 49(3): 461–475.

Hracs BJ, Jakob D and Hauge A (2013) Standing out in the crowd: The rise of exclusivity-based strategies to compete in the contemporary marketplace for music and fashion. *Environment and Planning A* 45(5): 1144–1161.

UNCTAD & UNDP. (2010) *Creative economy report 2010: Creative economy: A feasible development option*. United Nations, Geneva.

UNDP and UNESCO (2013) Creative economy report: Widening local development pathways. In: *Report prepared by Isar Y (ed)*. UNDP/UNESCO, Paris.

Wilson N, Gross J, Dent T et al. (2020) *Re-thinking inclusive and sustainable growth for the creative economy: A literature review*. Available at: https://disce.eu/wp-content/uploads/2020/01/DISCE-Report-D5.2.pdf (accessed 17/04/2020).

PART 1

Higher education and creative economies development

2 Creative higher education in Nigeria and the case of University of Lagos

Vincent Obia, Lauren England,
Roberta Comunian and Duro Oni

Introduction

The global attention on the creative economy has expanded in recent decades from the first definitions and mapping in Australia and in the United Kingdom (DCMS, 1998) to a broader global concentration (Reis, 2008). In particular, the focus of researchers and policymakers has moved from the Global North and East Asia to the Global South and the potential that the creative economy has for development (UNESCO, 2010, 2013). Furthermore, the understanding of the creative economy has expanded beyond its economic impact, to the uniqueness that creativity gives to other vocations/professions (Reis, 2008), and the relationship between creative economy and higher education (Comunian and Faggian, 2014; Comunian and Gilmore, 2016). Consequently, the creative economy is no longer just a collection of sectors, but a new economic cycle, a new dispensation, responding to global economic problems (Reis, 2008).

In Africa, there is little agreement on what the creative economy comprises, but stakeholders are usually of the view that it includes film/television/radio, performing art, music, visual art and animation, tourism and hospitality, arts and crafts, fashion and design, publishing, architecture and advertising (British Council, 2013). This has contributed to a problematic understanding of African cultural goods in response to the dynamics of the creative economy. Although cultural and creative industries (CCIs) have been identified as key to development in Africa, the reality on the ground does not portray this. For instance, with a few exceptions, there has been an absence of education programmes rooted in African culture and languages. One such exception is Babs Fafunwa who promoted an African culture and language-based education system through his work at the then University of Ife in 1957, arguing that this would aid comprehension (Oyelade, 2017). Others include secondary school projects such as the Olashore International School in Iloko, Osun

State which from inception in 1994 has focused on culture. Still, it is not unusual to find educational bodies in Nigeria today that are quick to adopt American or European curricula in schools. There is also a lack of social, economic and political policy systematically addressing the role to be played by stakeholders such as academia, the private sector and government in the creative economy (Reis, 2008). Although the Cultural Policy of Nigeria addresses some of these issues on a case-by-case basis, it does not reflect contemporary developments and implementation remains a problem.

Furthermore, the creative economy in Nigeria has not been streamlined as is noticeable in some developed countries. As a result, it remains opaque, informal and unstructured, with various sectors operating independently of one another (British Council, 2019; Miller, 2016). Regardless, the CCIs in Nigeria have shaped economic growth and led to employment generation (British Council, 2013). For instance, the film industry alone surpassed the US$3billion dollar mark in 2014 (Bright, 2015) and other sectors such as music and fashion have gained increasing traction (British Council, 2013). In 2014, Nigeria became the largest economy in Africa, mainly because Nollywood, the music industry and telecommunications were included in the rebased GDP calculation for the first time. By 2016, the arts, entertainment and recreation sector accounted for 2.3% of Nigeria's US$500billion+ GDP (PWC, 2017). Additionally, in 2019 the Central Bank of Nigeria introduced the Modalities for the Implementation of the Creative Industry Financing Initiative, a scheme meant to provide long-term, low-cost financing to entrepreneurs in the industry (CBN, 2019).

In this chapter we focus specifically on the role that education plays in the creative economy, highlighting the importance of HE. We use Nigeria and the University of Lagos as a case study but argue that more research is needed in other countries, and on other HE Institutions (HEIs) to highlight their role in the creative economy. The chapter builds on an extensive desktop data collection of courses across HEIs in Nigeria and includes qualitative findings and reflection from a focus group conducted in April 2019 at the University of Lagos with 15 representatives from a range of academic departments and courses. First, we review the education provision and policy framework in Nigeria with a focus on creative industries (CIs). We then turn to curriculum development and provision across Nigeria. Thereafter, we focus on Lagos and specifically the teaching and collaborative dynamics adopted by the University of Lagos to map opportunities and challenges for collaboration in the creative economy. Finally, we explore lessons learnt and avenues for future research.

Policy framework for creative industries and education in Nigeria

The National Cultural Policy was first developed in 1988 and the only subsequent review was unsuccessful, resulting in a 2008 draft cultural policy which is very similar to the original 1988 document. This suggests that the policy does not address the complexities and dynamics of the creative economy today, particularly as it relates to HE. In principle, the policy is based on the intrinsic value of culture focusing on national unity, pride, heritage and harmony (Asia, 2018; Culturelink, 1996; UNESCO, 2017). Thus, policy implementation focuses on the preservation, promotion and presentation of culture (Onyima, 2016) through education, the arts, literature, crafts, tourism and mobility within Nigeria.

Its administration and implementation rests with the Federal Department of Culture, while the National Council for Arts and Culture is saddled with the development of culture. Both agencies are supervised in their duties by the Ministry of Information and Culture (Culturelink, 1996). Various organisations, guilds and associations also exist in the CCIs, thereby solidifying the structure needed to promote the diversity of cultural expressions (UNESCO, 2017). The federating states also have various art councils which are set up by law, with a focus on the promotion of their distinct ethnic cultures (Culturelink, 1996).

Generally speaking, Nigeria participates in most international conventions relating to the creative economy and creative HE, and the cultural policy points to the link between culture, science and technology; cultural enterprises and CIs; and culture and education (UNESCO, 2017). On cultural enterprises and CIs, the policy emphasises strengthening craftsmanship, promoting the teaching of arts and crafts and the performing arts, and promoting the patronage of made in Nigeria goods such as textiles, all for economic impact. On culture and education, the policy advocates restructuring the total school environment to promote culture and creativity, addressing the challenges of modernisation, and providing training for professionals in the education sector.

Still, there are indications that the policy framework is unsystematic and incomprehensive. For instance, the Constitution (1999) empowers only the federal government to implement policies such as the cultural policy through the provision on Fundamental Objectives and Directive Principles of State Policy, thus impeding the ability of states to pursue policies of their own, despite having their own art councils (Asia, 2018). The highest law-making body in the country, the National Assembly, has also tried without success to harmonise bills on the Motion Picture Council of Nigeria (MOPICON) and the Theatre Arts Regulatory

Council (UNESCO, 2017), with implications for uncertainty and duplicity. The policy also lacks comprehensiveness as it recognises only publishing, broadcasting and film as CCIs (Culturelink, 1996). Even with this elementary recognition, the publishing sector has witnessed stunted growth associated with a lack of facilities and an overwhelming reliance on the production of school textbooks. With regards to film, policy treatment is superficial, glossing over the need for structures to address production and distribution (Culturelink, 1996).

Nevertheless, the major challenge is with implementation and funding. Thus far, little has been done to promote an educational system that stimulates ingenuity and supports creativity in the fields of arts, science and technology (Asia, 2018; Samuel and Chimeziem, 2009; UNESCO, 2017). Furthermore, a coordinated attempt at preserving the nation's cultural landscape, natural sites and monuments is lacking, and the culture sector has not been given sufficient attention in government circles (UNESCO, 2017).

The narrative regarding the educational policy framework in Nigeria is a little better but only in terms of the successful reviews that have been carried out over the years. The first notable summit on education was the National Curriculum Conference in 1969 which focused on universal free education and improved access to tertiary education. After this came the National Policy on Education (First 1977, Second 1981, Third 1988, Fourth 2004, Fifth 2007, and Sixth 2013). The 2013 review was aimed at making the citizen whole and to inculcate in him a national consciousness (NPE, 2013). It also assigns HEIs the responsibility of providing a more practical curriculum based on the needs of industry. Besides HEIs, the policy provides for vocational enterprise institutions (VEIs) in the areas of traditional fashion, craft, performing arts, make-up, art and contemporary fashion design for students who cannot make it to universities. The goal of VEIs is to make students think creatively and to provide practical training. The policy also provides for innovation enterprise institutions (IEIs) to cater for certification in industry-specific skills. The IEIs include the Fashion Institute of Technology, Film Academy, Academy of Creative Arts, Construction and Engineering Institute and other science-based and industrial institutions (NPE, 2013).

However, the goals of the 2013 review are vague. It does not recognise the need for STEAM (science, technology, engineering, art, and mathematics) or cross-cutting education. It delineates secondary education and places creative education in the humanities only, with little or no attempt to attach creativity to science and technology-based courses (see below for further discussion on HE context). It also fails to address issues such as policy somersaults, lack of policy implementation, poor teacher training and lack of capacity for skill training. Imam (2012) argues that the reviews of the education policy have led to an unstable educational system.

The creative economy has also not been sufficiently recognised in the Nigerian education system. Pre-1960s, the CCIs were neglected in favour of providing clerical training, and post-1960s, the attention shifted to producing manpower for economic expansion and the civil service (Adetoro, 2014). Today, the focus is on promoting science and technology education with little or no reference to the arts (Constitution, 1999). The educational policy draws from this emphasis and tilts heavily in favour of science education – 60% of HE admissions are reserved for science-based programmes, rising to 80% in the universities of technology or agriculture. Cultural and creative arts subjects are only compulsory in primary schools and become optional from then onwards (Imam, 2012), with fewer opportunities available for creative education as students progress in their educational pursuits.

Furthermore, the policy does not support creativity in HEIs; students are directed to consume theoretical knowledge rather than seeking new understandings, and teaching lacks connection with real-life problems, highlighting the disconnect between town and gown (Akinwale, 2008). Although the education policy provides for VEIs, Aderonmu (2012) identifies that vocational pursuits cannot be sustained because the policy does not promote enterprise. The education policy recognises a category of people as gifted in art, creativity, music, leadership and intellectual precocity and stipulates that specialist schools be created for them, but this has not been implemented.

Funding and training for teachers also remain key problems. For instance, the government has continually failed to meet the 26% budgetary allocation for education specified by UNESCO, despite this being captured in the education policy. The teaching profession remains unattractive (Babalola, 2013), and many go into teaching only to make ends meet or as a stepping stone to something greater. A lack of skilled teaching in primary and secondary schools further compounds challenges for creative academics in HEIs in addressing deficiencies in students' basic creative and cultural education.

Curriculum for creative higher education in Nigeria

Nigeria has always cherished the spectrum of arts, with importance attached to crafts such as painting, design, pottery, carving and dyeing (Mangiri, 2015). However, in the colonial days, art and creative education was relegated, subsumed into vocational training until painting was introduced in the 1920s (Onwuagboke, Singh and Fook, 2015). The first institutional recognition of the CCIs came in 1950 when art was introduced in Government College, Keffi, North-Central Nigeria, and in 1952 at the Yaba College of Technology in Lagos. This was followed in 1953 with the introduction of art in the Nigerian College of Art, Science and Technology in Ibadan, and other colleges in 1955. In 1960, the Ashby Report on the needs of HE in Nigeria called for art to be brought into mainstream education by making it compulsory. Thus, art disciplines were established in that decade at the University of Nigeria and the University of Ife (Mangiri, 2015). Today, it is common to find HEIs and other organisations dealing with the creative economy because of Nigeria's abundant creative talent (British Council, 2019).

HEIs are responsible for the curricula used in training creative workers, a responsibility conferred by the National Universities Commission through the Benchmark Minimum Academic Standard (BMAS). This document is meant to provide a concrete guide for HEIs in their choice of programmes and course modules. It focuses on theoretical knowledge, practical application and industrial experience, and prescribes a staff/student ratio of between 1:8 and 1:30 (National Universities Commission, 2007). In general, BMAS specifies 13 broad disciplines, out of which four are relevant to the creative economy – art, social sciences, environmental sciences, and engineering and technology – and this is also reflected in private universities (Covenant University Academic Handbook, 2014). While the discipline of art caters specifically to the creative economy, the other three contain relevant subjects outlined below.

In relation to the creative economy, the discipline of Art provides for the following courses: Languages and Literatures, Music, and Theatre/ Performing Arts (NUC Draft, 2015a). The Environmental Sciences discipline caters for Architecture, Fine Arts, and Industrial Design (NUC Draft, 2015b). Fine art specialisms include drawing, painting, sculpture, pottery, textile designs, illustrations, and graphic design. The Social Sciences discipline includes Mass Communication and Information Science/Media Studies (NUC Draft, 2015c). In mass communication, the specialisations provided include journalism, broadcasting, public relations, and advertising. Finally, the Engineering and Technology discipline incorporates Ceramic Engineering, Textile and Polymer Engineering, and Industrial Engineering (NUC Draft, 2015d).

While this highlights the potential for broad connections between HE and the creative economy, BMAS does not reflect cross-cutting education – the prevailing view is that technology can be used in teaching the arts, but never the other way round (Bolaji, 2007; NPE, 2013). There has also been inadequate response to the needs of contemporary societies and emerging new fields such as web design, games and animation, further compounding the problem of graduates not having the cutting-edge skills required (British Council, 2019). Hence, while more than half of those who work in the creative industry have some form of HE training (British Council, 2013), creative workers often have to seek self-training or on-the-job training to gain the skills needed to work in the industry (British Council, 2019; Culturelink, 1996). Industries such as Nollywood face major skill gaps because industry skills are not encouraged in a school system where the focus is on grades (British Council, 2019). Vocational education is also lacking in standardisation and official regulation or supervision (ibid).

Although BMAS specifies five-year periodic curriculum reviews, there is much to indicate that these reviews rarely take place, resulting in curricula that do not address new areas of specialisation (Magaji and Ilyasu, 2016). This is most notable in architecture (Aderonmu, 2012; Abdirad and Dossick, 2016). Notwithstanding the fact that BMAS specifies practical teaching, the lack of adaptation and advancement suggests a favouring of theoretical knowledge (Bolaji, 2007), although regular studios specifically targeted at practical teaching are held. For the arts, BMAS states that facilities such as equipment and rehearsals spaces be provided; still, funding remains a challenge (Agbowuro, Saidu and Jimwan, 2017).

Higher education provision in Nigeria

During our desktop mapping and databases research, we found 227 undergraduate courses in Nigeria at 104 university institutions (Table 2.1) covering CIs-related disciplines. We found that 32.6% of the courses are provided by private institutions and 67.4% are provided by public institutions. In all, we found that 52 public universities and 52 private universities offer courses in creative education in Nigeria.

The data also shows that private universities offer more courses in media and communication, while public universities offer more courses in performing arts. While public universities give considerable focus to fine and applied arts, it is curious that private universities do not provide for this course. But given that the line between fine arts and performing arts is blurred when it comes to HEIs in Nigeria, it is likely that some fine and applied arts courses are subsumed in the broader performing arts disciplines. We found that public universities also place more emphasis on design than private universities.

The South-West has more courses dealing with creative education, taking up 34.4% of the total number of courses (Table 2.2). In this region, Lagos and Osun have the most courses. This number points to

Table 2.1 Disciplines and undergraduate courses by university
types (incl. BA, BSc and BTech).

Creative field by University Type	Course Numbers	Percentage
Private University	**74**	**32.6**
Design (incl. Industrial Design)	1	0.4
Architecture	8	3.5
Performing Arts	12	5.3
Media & Communication	53	23.3
Public University	**153**	**67.4**
Music	3	1.3
Design (incl. Industrial Design)	5	2.2
Architecture	27	11.9
Fine & Applied Arts	35	15.4
Media & Communication	37	16.3
Performing Arts	46	20.3
Grand Total	**227**	**100.0**

the role that the South-West plays in creative education, particularly
Lagos, which is considered the art and commercial capital of Nigeria.
The South-South (22%) and South-East (21%) regions follow. The fig-
ures are much lower in the North, especially in the North-East (4%) and
North-West (7%). In the North-East, there are no entries for Jigawa and
Yobe states, and in the North-West, there are no entries for Katsina,
Sokoto and Zamfara states. These five are the only states missing in the
table. Table 2.2 shows the disparity between the North and the South of
Nigeria as far as creative education is concerned, with the South account-
ing for three-quarters of creative education courses in HEIs.

University of Lagos and the creative
economy: a case study

In this chapter, we use the case of the University of Lagos – specifically
the Faculty of Arts – to explore how universities engage with the creative economy and employability in relation to their creative graduates
(Comunian, Faggian and Jewell, 2014). The Faculty of Arts is one of
12 faculties at the University of Lagos. It started in 1964 as the School
of Humanities, two years after the University was established. In 1975,
this School was merged with the then School of African and Asian
Studies and re-designated Faculty of Arts. It comprises seven departments: Linguistics, African and Asian Studies, Creative Arts, English,
History and Strategic Studies, European Languages, Philosophy, and

Table 2.2 Course numbers and percentage by region/location (UG only).

Geo-Political Zone/Region	Location	Course Numbers	Percentage
North-West	Kaduna State	8	3.5
	Kano State	5	2.2
	Kebbi State	1	0.4
	Total	**16**	7.0
North-East	Adamawa State	4	1.8
	Bauchi State	2	0.9
	Borno State	2	0.9
	Taraba State	2	0.9
	Total	**10**	4.4
North-Central	Benue State	3	1.3
	Kogi State	3	1.3
	Kwara State	7	3.1
	Nasarawa State	4	1.8
	Niger State	2	0.9
	Plateau State	8	3.5
	Total	**27**	11.9
South-East	Abia State	5	2.2
	Anambra State	20	8.8
	Ebonyi State	5	2.2
	Enugu State	16	7.0
	Imo State	4	1.8
	Total	**51**	22.5
South-South	Akwa Ibom State	7	3.1
	Bayelsa State	3	1.3
	Cross River State	9	4.0
	Delta State	13	5.7
	Edo State	12	5.3
	Rivers State	8	3.5
	Total	**52**	22.9
South-West	Ekiti State	5	2.2
	Lagos State	12	5.3
	Ogun State	17	7.5
	Ondo State	8	3.5
	Osun State	16	7.0
	Oyo State	10	4.4
	Total	**78**	34.4
Federal Capital	Abuja	6	2.6
	Total	**6**	2.6
	Grand Total	**227**	100.0

Religious Studies. Of these, the Department of Creative Arts is of particular interest to us. The Department runs a four-year programme and has three arms: Theatre, Music, and Visual Arts. Visual Arts includes five specialisations: graphics, sculpture, ceramics, painting, and textile. Students who enrol in Creative Arts are grouped into one of the three arms from their first year, and those assigned to Visual Arts get to choose one of the five specialisations in their second year.

In April 2019, we held a focus group at the Department of Creative Arts which included 15 academics from across the university with participants from the Departments of Creative Arts, English, and Mass Communications. During the focus group we covered a range of topics under three broad headings: (1) how education connects and supports creative careers in Lagos, (2) how university research contributes to the creative economy and (3) how HEIs work with policy and what synergies they can develop. For the purpose of this chapter, we focus specifically on the first area of research.

The Department of Creative Arts says on their website:

> We are proud of our prosperous alumni engaged in the Nollywood and music industry as much as we can boast of artists that feature in major art exhibitions and biennales around the world. [...] This is 'The' Lagos Art School and one that showcases the best of Nigeria's culture in an atmosphere of rigorous research, innovation and design.

There is surely a broader pressure – common to probably all universities – to acknowledge the importance of supporting creative careers for their students. We articulate the data collected around three key topics: how CIs are brought into the campus and classes, how students are supported towards entering the creative sector externally, and what challenges and opportunities are currently developing in Lagos.

Bringing creative industries in …

In broad terms there is a strong input from industry into curriculum; experts from the sector are not only invited to comment on the content on offer, but also to give lectures and speak to the students on a regular basis. In more practical terms, the University of Lagos provides activities that promote opportunities for students to experience creative work and creative production. This includes the presence of a radio and TV station on campus where students are involved in presenting and preparing programmes and content:

They (students) are able to start practicing before they graduate. They are industry ready. Because, for instance, at Unilag (University of Lagos), they have one hour a day allocated to students to present programmes. So that's another way of getting them ready for the industry when they graduate. […] They are able to know how to use the camera, how to create programmes, how to present.

(Educator 3)

The educators found the students to be very proactive when experts visit them: "We find them taking selfies, they are asking for their complementary cards, their telephone numbers and all of that. And they keep in touch with them and you find a lot of them when they graduate, they're working with those people" (Educator 3). Furthermore, in providing experience for art students, the Department of Creative Arts recently started a new art gallery within their campus building (Lagoon Gallery, see Figure 2.1), not only showcasing the work of academics, but also allowing students to engage with gallery work and management.

Figure 2.1 The Lagoon Gallery, interior and exterior views (photos: R. Comunian).

... and taking students out

Many of the courses at the University of Lagos offer the opportunity for internships – also called attachments – which offer insights into creative work within a formal degree structure. The students spend six months in a related industry as part of their degree (the scheme is called Students Industrial Work Experience Scheme (SIWES) and was initiated by Duro Oni under the aegis of Creative Arts in Town).

> And a lot of them are able to get jobs when they graduate because they do so well when they go out during that period of internship, the attachments. They do so well that they work for them as soon as they graduate, you know, they grab them, and they offer them jobs, we have a lot of that happening.
>
> (Educator 2)

In the visual arts, students gained exposure by showing their work at the National Theatre and engaging with patrons, as well as connecting with potential funders in the sector. The connections academics have with the industry also allowed for more informal opportunities where industry partners simply ask educators to suggest a student to help on a production over their holiday or a summer break. They highlighted this as a synergy, especially with Nollywood and the entertainment industry, as it offered students valuable experience. However, we noticed the regulation (and potential reimbursement) of this work was not discussed or questioned in relation to issues of potential exploitation of recent graduates or current students. Some educators noted that these external opportunities also created challenges for the overall education programme, as it was hard to commit students' attention to educational work, given their eagerness to contribute to the sector.

Entrepreneurship education and start-ups

Like in many other international universities, the University of Lagos has recently invested in entrepreneurship programmes and spaces on campus. While this engages with the broader university agenda, it is specifically meaningful for the CIs sector (Ashton and Comunian, 2019). The Lagos academics seem to promote the rhetoric that students in the creative field can be more enterprising and create their own markets and career opportunities, as was identified by Comunian and Ooi (2016) in the case of Singapore.

> There's quite a lot of unemployment as you can tell in Nigeria. But what we try to do in the Department of Creative Arts is say,

"look, don't go looking for employment, you create that employment yourself".

(Educator 4)

This was despite an acknowledgement that "A lot of persons are interested either in the banking industry or in the oil companies and so on and so forth, not necessarily in arts" (Educator 5). The central investment of the university via the Research Office Support and Entrepreneurship Centre on campus (Figure. 2.2), coincidentally located just behind the Department of Creative Arts, seems an interesting new trajectory for these students. Emphasis was placed on supporting small business start-ups with potential to grow, and the potential exploitation of intellectual property.

And we are also as a Research Office interfacing with the Entrepreneurship Centre to see how some innovative business ideas could be potentially copyrighted. [...] Some business ideas that have

Figure 2.2 University of Lagos Entrepreneurship and Skill Development Centre (photos: R Comunian).

been found amongst the students can be quickly targeted and provided with some support in terms of having the small business unit, to getting started, […] the school is ready and very much willing to harness their potential by providing some support, no matter how little, it can go a long way in the end, and support entrepreneurs, people who can set up businesses in the future.

(Research Office Staff)

Conclusions: challenges and opportunities

The case study of the University of Lagos and the overview of the provision for creative HE across Nigeria present an interesting input on the role that universities play in the development and potential growth of local creative economies in Africa. However, this potential also comes with many challenges, as expressed by our focus group participants.

One of the main challenges is the societal view of being an 'artist'. Families do not see creative careers as sustainable for their young people and prefer to fund established academic pathways (law, medicine etc.) in the hope of having better sustainable incomes and career prospects after graduation. This is coupled with a view that the sector suffers from underinvestment, within and outside the education setting. This means that students and graduates often struggle to find resources, for example, affordable studio spaces to kickstart their careers. This connects also with the difficulties that both policy makers and investors have in seeing creative arts as a venture worth investment and fostering.

There are opportunities emerging for the sector with the Minister of Information and Culture, Lai Mohammed, in 2017 describing the CIs in Nigeria as its new oil, but these opportunities will require a coordinated approach, between industry, policy and academia. Overall, the submission of the focus group participants is at odds with the literature (Aderonmu, 2012; Akinwale, 2008; Asia, 2018; British Council, 2019; Culturelink, 1996). The participants suggest that HE has done well in shaping and providing talent for the creative economy, glossing over the shortcomings outlined in the literature. This suggests the need for further research based on the views of creative students, policymakers and creative experts.

References

Abdirad H and Dossick CS (2016) BIM curriculum design in architecture, engineering, and construction education: A systematic review. *Journal of Information Technology in Construction* 21: 250–271.

Aderonmu PA (2012) A framework for sustainable education in Nigeria: Strategies of re-integrating vocational skills into educational curriculum. Available at: http://eprints.covenantuniversity.edu.ng/3105/1/A%20Framework%20for%20Sustainable%20Education%20in%20Nigeria%20Strategies%20of%20Re-integrating.pdf (accessed 10 June 2019).

Adetoro RA (2014) Inclusive education in Nigeria – A myth or reality? *Creative Education* 5(20): 1777–1781.

Agbowuro C, Saidu S and Jimwan CS (2017) Creative and functional education: The challenges and prospects in a comatose economy. *Journal of Education and Practice* 8(8): 37–40.

Akinwale OB (2008) Promoting creativity in Nigeria. *Proceedings of the 1st National Engineering Technology Conference* 1: 370–375.

Ashton D and Comunian R (2019) Universities as creative hubs: Modes and practices in the UK context. In: Gill R, Pratt A and Virani T (eds) *Creative hubs in question: Place, space and work in the creative economy.* Cham: Palgrave Macmillan, pp. 359–379.

Asia EE (2018) Evaluating the provisions of cultural policy of Nigeria in the protection, preservation and promotion of Nigerian culture. Available at: https://www.academia.edu/37981768/EVALUATING_THE_PROVISIONS_OF_CULTURAL_POLICY_OF_NIGERIA_IN_THE_PROTECTION_PRESERVATION_AND_PROMOTION_OF_NIGERIAN_CULTURE_Importance_of_culture_and_imperatives_of_cultural_policy (accessed 10 June 2019).

Babalola J (2013) National teacher education policy in Nigeria within the context of global trends. Available at: https://www.academia.edu/22330818/NATIONAL_TEACHER_EDUCATION_POLICY_NTEP_IN_NIGERIA_WITHIN_THE_CONTEXT_OF_GLOBAL_TRENDS (accessed 15 June 2019).

Bolaji S (2007) Evolving creativity in Nigerian education: A philosophy paradigm. Available at: https://pesa.org.au/images/papers/2007-papers/bolaji2007.pdf (accessed 10 June 2019).

Bright J (2015) Meet Nollywood: The second largest movie industry in the world. Available at: http://fortune.com/2015/06/24/nollywood-movie-industry/ (accessed 7 July 2019).

British Council (2013) Mapping of Nigeria Creative Industries: Report of Lagos Pilot Study. British Council, Lagos https://www.britishcouncil.sl/sites/default/files/lagos_pilot_mapping_report_2013.pdf.

British Council (2019) Creative education and skills in Nigeria: A rapid analysis. Report, Federal Ministry of Information and Culture, Nigeria.

CBN (2019) *Modalities for the implementation of the creative industry financing initiative.* Abuja: Central Bank of Nigeria. Available at: https://www.cbn.gov.ng/out/2019/ccd/modalities%20for%20cifi%20implementation%20.pdf (accessed 4 July 2020).

Comunian R and Faggian A (2014) Creative graduates and creative cities: Exploring the geography of creative education in the UK. *International Journal of Cultural and Creative Industries* 1(2): 18–34.

Comunian R, Faggian A and Jewell S (2014) Embedding arts and humanities in the creative economy: The role of graduates in the UK. *Environment and Planning C: Government and Policy* 32(3): 426–450.

Comunian R and Gilmore A (eds) (2016) *Higher education and the creative economy: Beyond the campus.* Oxon: Routledge.

Comunian R and Ooi CS (2016) Global aspirations and local talent. *International Journal of Cultural Policy* 22(1): 58–79.

Constitution (1999) Constitution of the Federal Republic of Nigeria (Promulgation) No. 24. Abuja.

Covenant University Academic Handbook (2014) College of science and technology. Available at: http://eprints.covenantuniversity.edu.ng/3270/1/CoE%20H ANDBOOK.pdf (accessed 11 July 2019).

Culturelink (1996) Cultural policy in Nigeria. Available at: http://www.wwcd.org/policy/clink/Nigeria.html (accessed 10 June 2019).

DCMS (1998) Creative industries mapping document. Available at: https://ww w.gov.uk/government/publications/creative-industries-mapping-documents -1998 (accessed 10 June 2019).

Imam H (2012) Educational policy in Nigeria from the colonial era to the post-independence period. *Italian Journal of Sociology of Education* 1: 181–204.

Magaji M and Ilyasu MS (2016) The architectural education curriculum in the Nigerian schools of architecture. *IOSR Journal of Research Method in Education* 6(6): 13–17.

Mangiri SG (2015) Historical development of creative arts education in Nigeria. *Journal of Education, Arts and Humanities* 3(1): 6–10.

Miller J (2016) Labour in Lagos: Alternative global networks. In: Curtin M and Sanson K (eds) *Precarious creativity: Global media, local labour.* California: University of California Press, pp. 146–158.

National Universities Commission (2007) Benchmark minimum academic standards for undergraduate programmes in Nigerian universities. Abuja.

NPE (2013) *National policy on education* (6th ed). Abuja: NERDC.

NUC Draft (2015a) Benchmark minimum academic standards for undergraduate programmes in Nigerian universities – Art. Abuja.

NUC Draft (2015b) Benchmark minimum academic standards for undergraduate programmes in Nigerian universities – Environmental sciences. Abuja.

NUC Draft (2015c) Benchmark minimum academic standards for undergraduate programmes in Nigerian universities – Social sciences. Abuja.

NUC Draft (2015d) Benchmark minimum academic standards for undergraduate programmes in Nigerian universities – Engineering and technology. Abuja.

Onwuagboke BB, Singh TK and Fook FS (2015) Integrating technology in art education in Nigerian education system: The need for an effective pedagogical approach. *Mediterranean Journal of Social Sciences* 6(4): 184–192.

Onyima BN (2016) Nigerian cultural heritage: Preservation, challenges and prospects. *New Journal of African Studies* 12: 273–292.

Oyelade AF (2017) Aliu Babatunde Fafunwa's philosophy on education. *Makerere Journal of Higher Education* 9(1): 87–96.

PWC (2017) Spotlight: The Nigerian film industry. Available at: https://www.pwc .com/ng/en/assets/pdf/spolight-the-nigerian-film-industry.pdf (accessed 18 July 2019).

Reis AC (ed) (2008) *Creative economy as a development strategy: A view of developing countries*. Sao Paulo: Itau Cultural.

Samuel E and Chimeziem G (2009) Towards the implementation of the Nigerian cultural policy for the promotion of culture in Nigeria. *Creative Artist: A Journal of Theatre and Media Studies* 3(1): 201–210.

UNESCO (2010) Creative economy report 2010. Creative economy: A feasible development option. Report, United Nations, Geneva.

UNESCO (2013) Creative economy report 2013 special edition. Report, United Nations, Paris.

UNESCO (2017) Nigeria report: Diversity of cultural expression. Available at: https ://en.unesco.org/creativity/governance/periodic-reports/2017/nigeria (accessed 10 June 2019).

3 Collaborations for creative arts higher education delivery in Ghana

A case of the University of Cape Coast

Madinatu Bello

Introduction

The collaboration between higher education and the creative and cultural industries (CCIs) is becoming an area of growing interest for academics (Comunian and Gilmore, 2015; Comunian, Gilmore, and Jacobi, 2015) and policy bodies (UNCTAD and United Nations, 2008; UNESCO, 2006) internationally. However, the potential of these alliances and exchanges have not yet attracted the interest of researchers and policymakers in Africa. Despite the growing acknowledgements of the importance of the CCIs for cultural, social and economic development (Boccella and Salerno, 2016; Mandel, 2016; Oyekunle, 2015), there is little knowledge of how HE can facilitate or interconnect with this development and add to its potential. This is specifically the case in Ghana where collaboration appears opportunistic and conditional. From an academic viewpoint, collaboration serves the purpose of teaching and promotion. For the CCIs, it serves as an avenue for timely project completion and acquisition of coded and tacit knowledge.

Therefore, this chapter aims to contribute to this literature, looking at the case of Ghana, specifically at the University of Cape Coast (UCC) and its Department of Theatre Studies. The chapter is structured in four parts. Firstly, it reflects on the importance of higher education institutions (HEIs) and CCIs collaborations in the literature, with specific focus on the African and Ghanaian context. Then, the research methodology and chosen case study is outlined. Next, the findings are articulated under two headings: an overview of Creative Arts HE in Ghana and a discussion on modes and challenges of HEIs and CCIs collaboration in relation to the UCC case study. Finally, the conclusion reflects on the challenges hindering the effectiveness of existing collaboration.

The importance of collaboration between higher education and creative and cultural industries

The CCIs are increasingly becoming one of the relevant components of modern post-industrial economies due to their potential to generate income, wealth and employment (Comunian, Faggian, and Jewell, 2014; Gouvea and Vora, 2018). To sustain this potential, CCIs have turned to partnerships and collaborations with higher education institutions (HEIs) in order to create, disseminate and practice knowledge for sustainable economies. They create such partnerships to secure training and employment for students and graduates (Bridgstock and Cunningham, 2016; Comunian and Gilmore, 2016; Comunian, 2017) and most importantly to increase the responsiveness of their curricula offerings to industry needs (Gilmore and Comunian, 2016; Goddard and Vallance, 2013). Similarly, industries collaborate not only due to prospective workers, managers and other manpower needs but also to create opportunities for industry specialists to serve as speakers in academic trainings and as faculty hands-on training on industry facilities. Most importantly, it is to partner HEIs in the design, revision and implementation of curricula for teaching and learning (Ameyaw, Turnhout, Arts, and Wals, 2019; Tessema and Abejehu, 2017).

In Africa and specifically Ghana, rapid changes in society caused by digital technology and globalisation often create situations where some curricula in most HEIs are perceived to be obsolete by some critics and scholars (Akomolafe, 2019; Benade, 2016) or ascribed to the high level of graduate unemployment (Akomolafe, 2019). However, in the context of Ghana, scholarly research on such partnership and collaboration in creative arts appears to be absent. In the absence of such empirical documents, stakeholders continue to speculate on the gap between CCIs and their analogous departments in HEIs (Ghana News Agency, 2017). One of the many reasons cited for the gap, is that collaboration helps to rescue CCIs from collapsing and their analogous departments in HEIs from experiencing decline in student intake. As such, if CCIs are now on the verge of collapsing and departments in HEIs continue to experience low intake levels, then collaboration is absent (Hazell, 2020). Yet, a survey on the websites of some HEIs and CCIs reveals some forms of collaboration are present in mission statements, strategic plans, curricula and pedagogical approaches (see Academic Affairs Directorate of the Registrar's Offices, University of Ghana, 2014; Aryeetey, 2011; University of Cape Coast, 2015). Practitioners in work mostly deny such collaborations exist but do accept that they engage with colleagues for HEIs on personal levels to execute research projects. From the discussion so far, there appears to be a dilemma as to whether CCIs and HEIs in Ghana collaborate at all. The dilemma may be attributed to the many divergent views regarding the conceptualisation and operationalisation of the concept of partnership or collaboration in current discourse and what form the collaboration should take.

Methodology, data and case study

Research project and methodology

This chapter draws on part of my PhD research, started in 2017, which looks at the nature of collaboration between the CCIs and performing arts departments in universities in Ghana. The project aimed to address questions of what the current landscape of creative arts provision in Ghana is and what modes and means of collaborations with CCIs are used to strengthen this delivery. In order to answer the first research question, desktop and archival research was conducted on a selection of HEIs in Ghana. In order to address the second, a case study approach was adopted (Creswell, 2014; Neuman, 2014). The decision to select the Department of Theatre Studies at the University of Cape Coast was linked to pre-existing knowledge and access to the department. It was where I gained my bachelor's degree from, subsequently served as a service person and currently work as an Assistant Lecturer while pursuing my terminal degree at the Universitat Hildesheim. Furthermore, this case study has an interesting context because of its established collaborations with the National Theatre of Ghana, Roverman Productions and the Centre for National Culture, Cape Coast. Therefore, the project set out to explore the nature and form of curriculum collaboration between the Theatre Studies Department in UCC and selected CCIs in Ghana. Within the case study approach, further desktop and archival research was conducted along with qualitative semi-structured interviews and a focus group discussion (FGD). In all, three academics, three students (who attended the FGD), an academic/practitioner from the National Theatre of Ghana, a representative from Roverman Productions, the director of the Centre for National Culture (CNC) and the director of the Directorate of Research, Innovation and Consultancy, UCC participated in the study.

The Department of Theatre Studies, University of Cape Coast

The Department of Theatre Studies at UCC is situated within the Faculty of Arts, which was one of the first faculties established when the university became a University College in 1962. The university is located in

Cape Coast, the capital of the Central region of Ghana. It was established out of the need for highly qualified and skilled human resource capital for education who had the capacity to meet the manpower needs of other ministries and industries in the country and beyond. It is also situated within one of the best hubs for tourism promotion in the country, thus, creating opportunity for the sustenance of CCIs which abound in the city (University of Cape Coast, 2015). The Faculty comprises nine departments, a centre, a unit and an institute: Theatre and Film Studies, Music and Dance, English, Communication Studies, Ghanaian Languages and Linguistics, Classics and Philosophy, French, History, Religion and Human Values, Information Literacy Unit, Institute of African and International Studies, and Confucius Centre (University of Cape Coast, 2015). The focus here is on the Theatre Studies Department and the synergies it creates with CCIs institutions within and beyond the academic domain for its teaching activities.

The department runs a four-year degree programme in theatre with nine specialisations: Performing Arts Management, Theatre for Development, Playwriting, Directing, Acting, Drama in Education, Scenic Design and Construction, Lighting Design and Construction, and Costume and Make-up Design and Construction. Students enrol on the Bachelor of Arts taking the Theatre Studies programme with two other cognate courses in the Faculty, which are dropped to concentrate on theatre at the third year of the programme. A theatre major student is mandated to specialise and graduate in one of the aforementioned areas together with other compulsory courses from the third year. According to the 50th Vice Chancellor's Annual Report in 2017, the department seeks to provide an institutional context for contemporary research that is not only valuable for its intrinsic purpose of creating and sharing knowledge, but also to research that impacts teaching and learning in progressive ways. The department also endeavours to integrate theory with practice and to motivate students to find connections between what they learn in school and real-life experiences. This demonstrates, then, that the department is interested in collaboration beyond the teaching environment (University of Cape Coast, 2015).

Creative arts higher education in Ghana

According to Newman and Duwiejua (2015) and Kamran, Liang and Trines (2019), the HE landscape in Ghana comprises three colleges of agriculture, 11 nursing training institutions, 38 colleges of education, ten polytechnics (eight now upgraded to technical universities), ten public universities and 63 private tertiary institutions. All training colleges since

2018 have been upgraded to university colleges and as such offer a four-year Bachelor of Education degree which is initially awarded by UCC and later by other affiliated public universities (Kamran et al., 2019). This chapter focuses on all public universities and three private universities because most creative arts education, especially theatre education, takes place only at the university level. Theatre education is categorised under performing arts education. Curricula for creative arts education in Ghana encompasses visual arts and performing arts at the basic level Junior High School (JHS) and Secondary High School (SHS) level. At the JHS level, the visual arts component comprises vocational skills, technical drawing and technical skills. Visual arts and clothing and textiles are creative arts subjects at the SHS level. At the JHS level, performing arts are included in the curriculum as part of cultural studies while at SHS, they are more informal or act as extracurricular activity.

The HEIs in Ghana have no national curriculum. Curricula for the provision of creative arts HE are left to the discretion of HEIs. Consequently, creative arts curricula are developed, delivered and assessed differently but with a similar vision. The performing arts discipline in general is engaged with producing graduates that will contribute to the human resource needs of the sector at different levels. They achieve this through their creative productions, seminars, conferences, workshops and scholarly works which create avenues for sharing ideas among practitioners, academics and students (Academic Affairs Directorate, University of Ghana, 2014; University of Cape Coast, 2015). In spite of this major similarity, creative arts programme credential names and composition differ from one HEI to another. For example, the School of Performing Arts at University of Ghana offers programmes including Music, Dance and Theatre Arts with a final certification of Bachelor of Fine Arts, Bachelor of Arts (Theatre Arts or Dance Studies or Music) and Bachelor of Music (Academic Affairs Directorate, University of Ghana, 2014). The University of Cape Coast and University of Education, Winneba (UEW) offer Bachelor of Theatre Studies but with different programme composition. In addition, UCC has Bachelor of Music, Bachelor of Arts (Music) Bachelor of Arts (Dance) and Bachelor of Arts (Film Studies) programmes while UEW has Music Education. Both institutions offer vocational and technical education with specialisations in clothing and textiles, communication design, sculpture and painting.

Programmes in these disciplines are taught from theoretical and practical perspectives. Pedagogical methods differ from one academic to the other but predominantly use the teaching methods of lectures, project-based and problem-based fieldtrips, community participatory projects, practical productions and seminars (Kamran et al., 2019; University of

Cape Coast, 2015). Assessment procedures include but are not limited to tests, assignments, oral presentations, practical presentations, final project theses, long essays and field reports (Kamran et al., 2019). Despite a practical nature to these programmes, space, logistics, equipment and a limited number of academics create challenges for their delivery.

A cursory look at the websites of the various public and private universities reveals that 17 public and one private HEI run creative arts programmes. The 18 institutions comprise 14 public universities which run 60 creative arts programmes and four private universities which also run seven creative arts programmes as represented in Table 3.1.

As evidenced in Table 3.1, public universities offer more programmes in design and performing arts while the four private universities offer more communication-related programmes. The number of performing arts programmes offered in public HEIs is more encouraging compared to that of private universities. Nonetheless, the number is far less compared to programmes in design. Considering the emphasis of Ghanaian cultural policy towards the CCIs as well as creative arts promotion for sustainability, performing arts programmes might need to expand to other institutions (National Commission on Culture, 2004).

Table 3.1 Undergraduate creative arts programmes in accredited universities in Ghana.

Creative Field by University Types	Programme Numbers	Percentage
Public University	60	89.6
Performing Arts	8	11.9
Communication Studies	4	6.0
Communication Design	2	3.0
Technology Design	17	25.4
Fine/ Applied Arts	11	16.4
Music Education	1	1.5
Art Education	7	10.4
Architecture	5	7.5
Culture & Tourism	4	6.0
Film & Media	1	1.5
Private University	7	10.4
Communication Studies	3	4.5
Architecture	1	1.5
Technology design	1	1.5
Performing Arts	2	3.0
Grand Total	67	100.0

Source: Author's data.

Collaborations in theatre education: informality and permeability in and outside campus

Nature of collaborations in curriculum design and implementation

The analysis of interviews reveals that collaborations between academic staff, students and the CCIs were more informal, of individual and departmental initiatives, vertical in nature and often short-term. There was rarely formal memorandums of understanding (MoU) or contracts signed between the Department and any of these CCIs as indicated by one of the participants.

> I will say that structurally we don't have such a formal linkage with the industry players. Officially we don't have but individually, we have some [...] faculty who are engaged constantly with the industry in terms of performances.
>
> (Participant, Academic 3)

Such collaborations established on mutual friendships that individuals created with people in industry either through networking from previous performance engagements and events or with colleagues from previous educational institutions reinforce the work of Kreiner and Schultz (1993). A participant from CNC said the following about collaborations.

> We collaborate but it's not like we've written them down [...]. We don't sit down to sign any MoU [...] they normally send a request by word of mouth or by text message [...]. We understand ourselves. We had been colleagues at the university or friends from conferences or workshop, so why an official contract before a collaboration.
>
> (Participant, CNC)

Critically, such informal collaboration highlights the pursuance of non-guided forms of written agreement or contractual agreement (Ankrah and AL-Tabbaa, 2015). It suggests the dominance of specific and complex exchanges and reciprocity guided by trust, needs and respect. Some participants from the Theatre Studies Department confirmed this when they indicated that most of their industry colleagues collaborated with were former university colleagues or friends whom they could trust and rely on in times of need for any collaborative scheme.

> I call on them either to visit their workplace with my students or for them to come to campus to interact with them [...]. That is a personal initiative for my teaching not something the Department

does [...]. They do respond to my calls because they know I will do same if they call on me.

(Participant, Academic 2)

The only aspect which might be ascribed to formality might be with the letters which students and staff presented to these sector partners as staff and students moved in to interact with CCIs as part of the teaching and learning processes. Written MoUs recorded by the Department were with other local universities and international non-governmental organisations like UNICEF and the Canadian International Development Agency (CIDA). This form of collaboration is termed 'focused structures' (Ankrah and AL-Tabbaa, 2015).

The findings further highlight that individual collaborations dominated departmental collaborations. Both academic and industry participants acknowledged that they forged individual collaborations with colleagues and staff rather than at a departmental or institutional level. The collaborations were to help meet set targets in teaching, learning, research and industrial projects. One participant from CNC indicated:

> unofficially and on individual interactions that is what I will say there has been certain contributions [...]. the centre organised the maiden edition of the "Performing Arts Forum" and during that programme, we had to partner academics [...]. They also assisted us in understanding the scope if we should talk about "Performing Arts Forum", the kind of scope that we should capture and all that.
>
> (Participant, CNC)

Though personal and informal, this form of collaboration, according to Ankrah and AL-Tabbaa (2015), is more efficient because it is based on trust between the parties involved. It also relegates or overcomes bureaucratic processes that may hinder the establishment of such partnerships. Another participant from the National Theatre of Ghana stated:

> I call on [...] [name withheld] when I need him to help me execute any project. At times, if you want to use the formal way, that is, write to the department for approval, the bureaucracies will delay the whole project. So I prefer to call on him so that we do everything quick.
>
> (Participant, National Theatre)

For the academics, personal collaboration with CCIs was for personal development in academia outside of its value in enhancing teaching and outreach programmes. Collaborations then became ways to gain access to individual expertise to facilitate projects, acquire logistics to enhance teaching, gain access to performance spaces for teaching, assess practical courses and serve as platforms for experts/practitioners from the CCIs to interact with students (Ahamed Galib, Nahar Munny, and Khudaykulov, 2015; Wearing, 2013).

The only formal departmental collaboration with CCIs in existence between 2014 and 2016 was that with CNC. Prior to that, the Department had secured an informal collaboration with a television station, Coastal Television, in Elmina, which ended as the television station began to gradually lose its place in the city. The collaboration with CNC (2014–2016) created an environment for academics to access facilities (and even human resources) for staff and students' theatre performances. This was particularly valuable as the Department did not have access to the formal university auditorium at that time. Such collaboration allowed for a discount on the rental charges for the performance space at CNC and minor collaborative schemes. This practice stopped when the university provided spaces for the department's productions and became aware of the costs associated with the use of CNC. Management was compelled to pay for the cost of the CNC auditorium because practical performances within the Department formed part of students' semester assessments and ultimately their total assessment at the end of their fourth year.

In addition, findings from the analysis indicate collaborations were often short-term. They ended when one of the actors ceased to be part of it or had achieved their goal. One of the academic participants confirmed this when he stated:

> Mostly, the collaboration I have with colleagues from the industry formally ends when the project is completed or when I finish teaching for the semester. But, informally, we still keep on contacting each other so that if any "galamsey", you know what I mean [...] private projects surface, then I'm quickly invited. You see, we need to create networks.
>
> (Participant, Academic 2)

A change in management also affected or ended departmental collaboration in particular. This happened where existing collaborations were contrary to the views of incoming directors and academic heads. This was confirmed by participants from both sectors. One academic stated:

> I think at one point, I suggested to the [...] the HOD that why we don't have a link with Centre for National Culture where for

example we can have our acting classes there [...]. So it wasn't an official collaboration and official linkage so when he left office, we had to come back to our old domain.

(Participant, Academic 1)

Hierarchies and managing collaborations

The findings also showed that these collaborations were often hierarchical and as such, involved power dynamics. For example, the Theatre Studies Department, from its inception, controlled the design and review of its curriculum and larger aspects of its implementation. They mainly did not involve their counterparts in industry at the conception, planning stage or implementation stage. Comunian (2017) refers to such "power dynamics" in collaboration when she argues that due to the huge nature of university structures, it is likely that the university will mostly lead collaborative agendas between them and organisations in the creative economy, setting the "terms and conditions and framework for the collaboration" (p. 236). To this end, academics almost always design and review programmes to meet the expected benchmarks of the National Accreditation Board (NAB) in Ghana. According to participants from the university, structures and policies within the university, guidelines from National Council for Tertiary Education (NCTE) and NAB defined and regulated who designed and delivered curricula and therefore limited the opportunities for external partners to contribute. This meant that practitioners in the CCIs were in no way included in the Department's curriculum design and implementation processes as stated by one of the academics and confirmed by a participant from the CCIs.

I've never seen anyone from the industry sit in a review of our curriculum [...]. I think there's some kind of maybe we'll say, parallel lines. We are both in parallel lines.

(Participant, Academic 3)

They (academics) normally come to us with requests for technical resources to lecture their students or for human resources for further explanations to what they teach the students [...]. I'm able to go there to teach and make inputs to the curriculum maybe because I double as a lecturer in another university and as a practitioner here.

(Participant, National Theatre)

The limitation of who can design, inform and implement university curricula was also reinforced by a participant from the Directorate of Research, Innovation and Consultancy (DRIC-UCC) who indicated that more often than not universities are bound by benchmarks from NAB and NCTE which are also informed by policies from external institutions like the World Bank, International Monetary Fund (IMF), United Nations Educational, Scientific and Cultural Organization (UNESCO) and United Nations Development Programme (UNDP). Academic qualification and expertise constituted major criteria that delineate who designed and implemented every curriculum in the university.

Consequently, the Department's curriculum and course contents, according to some participants from the CCIs, rarely reflected their practices and activities. A large portion of content often referred to by academics as 'best international practices' was in fact representational of practices from the Global North. These "best practices", most participants conceded, hardly thrived in the Ghanaian context because of the logistics and at times, lack of them, posing challenges to the realisation of the course content and in turn affecting the level of expertise of graduates. The few courses that reflected industry activities took place in the classroom with field trips (once a year) but without guest lecturers from the industry.

Interestingly, government recruitment policies coupled with rigid university structures posed challenges to the Department, constraining its ability to recruit experts (persons without preferred qualification) from firms to augment the seemingly under-resourced human resources. This implied a more theoretical approach to teaching and learning within such a practical oriented programme. Despite the efforts made by these academics, these challenges appeared to deflate the quality of graduates that are prepared for the industry because knowledge and practice from the university appeared to be at variance with existing norms and practices in the job market. One participant in the FGD who was a student attested to this.

> we are always on campus, no workshops are being organised by the department for us to get to know those who are in the industry and then learn new techniques or the new ways of doing things, and it's like, it's all about the book [...]. When we go home and we go for internship or attachment, it's as if we know nothing [...]. At times I ask myself if I can get a job after completion.
>
> (FGD Participant, Student B)

Forms of collaboration on and off campus

Collaboration in teaching at the Theatre Studies Department exists informally but not in curriculum design as previously highlighted. From the findings, it is evident that individual lecturers invited colleagues from the CCIs to act as guest lecturers for some topics in the courses they taught. This was not on a regular basis because of challenges regarding funding for such invitations. However, the student association attached to the Department (Association of Students of Performing Arts) complemented the efforts of academics by organising workshops and programmes which brought people from the CCIs to campus.

> Basically it's not the department which organised this programme but I think the department should organise more of such programs; seminars and invite people but it shouldn't target only the theatre student, we can also target other students so that they can also come and understand [what theatre is].
>
> (FGD participant, Student B)

Based on what most of the students who took part in the FGD said, such collaborations provided them with the chance to meet with people from the CCIs and create links and networks which would act as catalysts for them securing jobs after graduation. They, therefore, advocated for more of such collaborations such as workshops, guest lectures and seminars.

Collaborations which took students and lecturers off campus took the forms of internships, attachments, field trips and students' research projects. In most cases, students' internship and attachment initiatives were informal. They were initiated by the students who displayed an enthusiasm to gain sector experience. They engaged in these activities in order to update their skills and knowledge in the arts and to be able to meet future industry requirements. One of the students claimed:

> sometimes going for classes and having the courses in theory, we think we understand but we go out there into the industries and then we see a more practical version of it then we realise that our understanding was totally different.
>
> (FGD participant, Student A)

Field trips were usually organised by individual lecturers based on what they planned to teach for the semester. This happened mostly for students in the third and final year majoring in areas like Performing Arts Management, Costume and Make-up and Scenic Design and Construction. In all, although most of the academics did not organise such interactions for students, they encouraged them to establish such collaborations on their own. Programmes that were initiated by the student association created enabling situations for students to easily get placements for internships and attachments. For example, collaborations with Roverman Productions were mostly initiated by the students' association and enabled students to create rapport with the director and producer. With such a rapport, most students were able to gain internships with that organisation which would have been difficult otherwise.

Conclusion

The chapter aimed to reflect on HE and CCIs collaboration in the context of Ghana. It presented the case study of the Theatre Studies Department of UCC to reflect on the practices and modes of collaboration, in and outside the campus, as well as the challenges faced by the HE sector and students wanting to engage with CCIs for their future careers. Curriculum design and implementation within the discourse of academia–industry collaboration have received attention in recent times especially in developing economies where universities are beginning to embrace new and evolving ideas from their colleagues in industry (Abebe Assefa, 2016). Unfortunately, achieving robust curriculum collaboration appears to lag behind research collaboration due to lack of trust, poor leadership and differences in institutional cultures (Abebe Assefa, 2016). This lag has created the assumption that there are no partnerships between academics and practitioner in the field of work. In fact, these collaborations are informal, mostly from individual's rather departmental initiative. They also tend to be quite hierarchical and short-term collaborations. Despite the shortcomings characterising these collaborations, most participants acknowledged some positive effects these collaborations had had on human resource development, student training and ultimately, on the growth and development of both sectors. However, most participants advocated the need for more formal frameworks for collaborations in addition to the informal ones. They further proposed that existing ones needed to be constantly reviewed and strengthened. Some of the participants (both academics and field practitioners) proposed that NCTE, NAB and university management should review policy restrictions and bureaucratic structure in favour of more collaborative relations.

This chapter is based on an individual departmental case study and further research could be conducted across Ghana to gain a wider perspective on whether these issues are shared. However, with the engagement of the broader creative arts HE sector and their CCIs partners, national policy could drive all stakeholders to redefine their mandate and strategies in the promotion, conservation and dissemination of performing arts activities in order to truly contribute to the broader agenda for the cultural development stipulated by *The Cultural Policy of Ghana* (National Commission on Culture, 2004).

Bibliography

Abebe Assefa, A. (2016). University-industry linkage practices, determinants and challenges theoretical and empirical article review: Lessons for effective and successful collaboration. *International Journal of Research in Management, 6*(3), 1–16.

Academic Affairs Directorate of the Registrar's Offices, University of Ghana, Legon. (2014). *University of Ghana Strategic Plan 2014–2024.* Academic Management Committee, NAFTI.

Ahamed Galib, M., Nahar Munny, K., & Khudaykulov, A. (2015). Enhancing university–industry collaboration: What are the drivers of academic researchers' involvement in industry? *International Journal of Innovation and Economic Development, 1*(1), 36–46.

Akomolafe, D. (2019). Obsolete curriculum responsible for unemployment. *Vanguard,* 27 September.

Ameyaw, J., Turnhout, E., Arts, B., & Wals, A. (2019). Creating a responsive curriculum for postgraduates: Lessons from a case in Ghana. *Journal of Further and Higher Education, 43*(4), 573–588.

Ankrah, S., & AL-Tabbaa, O. (2015). Universities–industry collaboration: A systematic review. *Scandinavian Journal of Management, 31*(3), 387–408.

Aryeetey, E. (2011). *Vice Chancellor's Annual Report 2011.* Accra: University of Ghana.

Benade, L. (2016). Is the classroom obsolete in the twenty-first century? *Educational Philosophy and Theory, 49*(8), 796–807.

Boccella, N., & Salerno, I. (2016). Creative economy, cultural industries and local development. *Procedia: Social and Behavioral Sciences, 223,* 291–296.

Bridgstock, R., & Cunningham, S. (2016). Creative labour and graduate outcomes: Implications for higher education and cultural policy. *International Journal of Cultural Policy, 22*(1), 10–26.

Comunian, R. (2017). Creative collaborations: The role of networks, power and policy. In M. Shiach & T. Virani (Eds.), *Cultural Policy, Innovation and the Creative Economy* (pp. 231–244). London: Palgrave Macmillan UK.

Comunian, R., Faggian, A., & Jewell, S. (2014). Embedding arts and humanities in the creative economy: The role of graduates in the UK. *Environment and Planning C: Government and Policy, 32*(3), 426–450.

Comunian, R., & Gilmore, A. (2015). *Beyond the Creative Campus: Reflections on the Evolving Relationship Between Higher Education and the Creative Economy.* London: King's College London.

Comunian, R., & Gilmore, A. (2016). *Higher Education and the Creative Economy: Beyond the Campus*. London and New York: Routledge.

Comunian, R., Gilmore, A., & Jacobi, S. (2015). Higher education and the creative economy: Creative graduates, knowledge transfer and regional impact debates. *Geography Compass*, *9*(7), 371–383.

Creswell, J. W. (2014). *Research Design: Qualitative, Quantitative, and Mixed Methods Approach* (4th edn.). California: Sage Publications.

Ghana News Agency. (2017). Education experts call for partnership between industry and academia. *Citifmonline.com*. http://citifmonline.com/2017/11/edu cation-experts-call-for-partnership-between-industry-and-academia/ (Accessed June 1, 2019).

Gilmore, A., & Comunian, R. (2016). Beyond the campus: Higher education, cultural policy and the creative economy. *International Journal of Cultural Policy*, *22*(1), 1–9.

Goddard, J., & Vallance, P. (2013). *The University and the City* (M. Feldman, G. Grabher, R. Martin, & M. Perry, Eds.) (First). New York: Routledge, Taylor and Francis Group.

Gouvea, R., & Vora, G. (2018). Creative industries and economic growth: Stability of creative products exports earnings. *Creative Industries Journal*, *11*(1), 1–32.

Hazell, C. (2020). How to increase adult students enrolment through organisational partnership. *Abound.college*.

Kamran, M., Liang, Y., & Trines, S. (2019). Education in Ghana. *World Education News + Reviews*, 16 April.

Kreiner, K., & Schultz, M. (1993). Of networks across organizations. *Organization Studies*, *14*(2), 189–209.

Mandel, B. (2016). From "serving" public arts institutions to creating intercultural contexts: Cultural management in Germany and new challenges for training. *Encatc Journal of Cultural Management & Policy*, *6*(1), 12.

National Commission on Culture. (2004). *The Cultural Policy of Ghana* (M. Ben Abdallah, Ed.) (First). Accra: Afram Publications.

Neuman, L. W. (2014). *Social Research Methods: Qualitative and Quantitative Approaches. Pearson New International Edition*. Harlow: Pearson Education Limited.

Newman, E., & Duwiejua, M. (2015). Models for Innovative Funding of Higher Education in Africa – The Case in Ghana. In P. Okebukola (Ed.), *Towards Innovative Models for Funding Higher Education in Africa* (pp. 1–109). Accra: Association of African Universities Press.

Oyekunle, O. (2015). Building the creative industries for sustainable economic development building the creative industries for sustainable economic development in South Africa. *International Journal of Sustainable Development*, 7(12), 47–72.

Tessema, B. S., & Abejehu, S. B. (2017). University-industry collaboration in curriculum development: Analysis of banking and finance graduates' attributes from educators and industries perspective. *Education Journal*, *6*(2), 87–93. https://doi.org/10.11648/j.edu.20170602.13.

UNCTAD, & United Nations. (2008). Creative economy outlook and country profiles: Trends in international trade in creative industries. *Harvard Business Review, 8*(9), 74.

UNESCO. (2006). *Understanding Creative Industries: Cultural Statistics for Public-Policy Making.*

University of Cape Coast. (2015). *50th Vice Chancellor's Annual Report.* University of Cape Coast Press.

Wearing, D. P. (2013). *Inter-Institutional Collaboration in the New Zealand Tertiary Education Sector.* PhD Thesis, Southern Cross University, Australia.

4 Fashion designers and education in Nairobi

Challenges and opportunities

Lauren England, Ogake Mosomi, Roberta Comunian and Brian J. Hracs

Introduction

The academic literature widely acknowledges that higher education (HE) plays an essential role in the development of the creative economy (Comunian et al., 2015). However, we still need a better understanding of how this value can be articulated within specific sub-sectors of the creative and cultural industries (CCIs) (England, 2020; Faggian et al., 2013). Although the relationship between the creative economy and HE have recently become a focus of attention (Comunian and Gilmore, 2016), these studies and reports tend to lump creative sectors together. However, we know that the structures, demands and imperatives of different CCIs are often unique. Some sectors adopt more structured business models and career pathways (for example architecture and software) while others rely more on flexible arrangements and freelance work (England, 2020; Faggian et al., 2013). Moreover, it is crucial to consider the complexity of how creative subjects might be taught differently in different national frameworks for education. Within this broader landscape, this chapter focuses specifically on fashion and the role of HE in the fashion design sector in Nairobi and Kenya more broadly.

In particular, we investigate the opportunities that education can offer in developing a more robust fashion design sector in Nairobi. As argued by Tuigong et al. (2015: 520), the textile and apparel industry holds "the highest potential of fostering Africa's export competitiveness and export-led pro-poor growth by generating greater employment due to its relative labour-intensiveness". However, we argue most researchers in this area focus on the importance of (mass) production for Kenyan textile and apparel development, without considering the importance of original content creation and fashion design, where education can also play an important role.

The chapter builds on fieldwork and data collection undertaken in Nairobi, Kenya during September 2019. It uses both quantitative and qualitative data to investigate what courses and education level fashion designers working in Nairobi attended, and how education and career opportunities might attract them to the capital city. It also includes qualitative reflections collected across ten focus group discussions with local Nairobi designers.

Firstly, we provide a brief introduction to fashion as an economic and creative sector in Kenya. Secondly, we introduce some of the literature on HE and the creative economy, looking specifically at the challenges of creative education. We then review the education provision and policy framework of HE and fashion design education in Kenya. After mapping the current provision and reflecting on curriculum development in Nairobi, we present our own research methodology and focus our analysis on findings from an online survey and focus group discussions relating to education and early career development. Here we identify the role of HE as a key provider of creative human capital for the fashion sector, and consider the education and training provided in relation to the demands and needs of industry. In the conclusions, we reflect on the role HE can and needs to play in developing value-adding opportunities in fashion and textiles, and reconnecting with broader developmental goals and agendas which might influence the sector's next stage of development in Kenya.

The Kenyan fashion industry: from ashes to phoenix?

The Kenyan textile industry was an essential sector for the country's industrial development in the 1990s. However, in the following decades, with the impact of globalisation and the rise of Asian production and exports, its role and production volumes have radically declined (Maiyo and Imo, 2012). Many authors highlight how apparel production in Kenya has suffered from global pressure and competition (Mastamet-Mason and Kachieng'a, 2009). In particular, Kobia et al. (2017) argue that beyond cheaper imports from East Asia, second-hand clothing from the West has caused a slowdown in the development of both skilled labour and new talent, especially following the renewal of the African Growth and Opportunity Act (AGOA) in 2015. Amongst East African countries, Kenya and Ethiopia are signposted to become prominent players in garment manufacturing (Berg et al., 2015). However, this is often understood in a reductionist way: as countries "leading emerging garment suppliers for high volume bulk basics" (ibid.: 1). Instead, it is essential to consider how fashion can align with broader policy strategies which connect with production but could also go beyond this. For example, fashion and creative courses could feature more broadly in Kenya's 2030 strategy. However, the document instead emphasises that "Kenya aims at expanding access to university education from 4.6% to 20%, with an emphasis on science and technology courses" (Government of Kenya, 2008: 11). Overall, more broadly, fashion and the CCIs are not included in the strategy despite an emphasis on "moving the Economy Up the Value Chain" (ibid.: 5). Fashion is discussed simply concerning manufacturing and "creating new high-value niche products e.g., cultural, eco-, and water-based tourism" (ibid: 5). Yet, Maiyo, Rael, and Imo highlight that an essential step in revitalising and adding value to the textile sector is to review "training courses in relevant institutions to meet industry needs and increase human development and training" (2012: 1). Similarly, Hivos and Equity Bank (2016) discuss the critical role played by training and education to strengthen the value created by local fashion designers and small tailoring houses to develop and integrate the Clothing to Fashion Value Chain.

Creative education and fashion education: challenges and career sustainability

HE has a longstanding relationship with the economy (Yorke, 2006), including the creative economy, in the development of human capital, networks, research, partnerships and knowledge and providing hard and soft infrastructure to support economic development (Comunian and Faggian, 2011; Comunian and Gilmore, 2015). More recently, however, the HE system (Boden and Nedeva, 2010), including creative education (Houghton, 2016), has become closely tied to a skills agenda (More and Moreton, 2017). Yorke (2006: 8) defines employability as "a set of achievements – skills, understandings and personal attributes – that makes graduates more likely to gain employment and be successful in their chosen occupations, which benefits themselves, the workforce, the community and the economy". This is associated with a growing 'enterprise culture' in HE and ongoing marketisation following neoliberal policies (Olssen and Peters, 2005). In the case of the UK, McRobbie (2016) suggests that the increased emphasis on graduate employability in the CCIs arises from the provision of most training – vocational, technical and academic – under the umbrella of the university. However, the situation is different in other countries. There has been widespread criticism of a skills gap between the content of education and training and the demands of industry (Moore and Morton, 2017). This critique has been particularly strong in CCI sectors (Frenette and Tepper, 2016), where programmes are positioned as failing to deliver graduates with the skills needed by and for industry. This challenge is also connected to rapid changes taking place in industries like fashion (McKinsey, 2019) and therefore the difficulty for the HE system in keeping up.

Employability and fashion

In the context of fashion, Kamaul et al. (2013: 29) suggest that that "employability of fashion and garment making youth polytechnic graduates is dependent not on mastery on vocational skills alone, but more so in the adequacy of occupational, empowerment and interpersonal and transferable skills". The need for 'real-world' experience and education *in* enterprise for fashion designers (Mills, 2011) is echoed in studies on a range of creative specialisms (Ashton, 2016). It is also important to consider how creative curricula can be flexible to accommodate broader challenges and nuances of fashion as a global sector such as "expanding global markets, sub-cultures, available resources, and technologies" (Faerm, 2012: 212). This chapter reflects on how fashion education aims to balance the importance of vocational knowledge with broader skills that enable fashion designers to enter and succeed in the sector.

There is also an issue with increasingly intense competition in the creative economy (Brydges and Hracs, 2019). Furthermore, the pressure for graduates to be 'work-ready' and to enter their field immediately as professionals may be unrealistic (England, 2020). Caves (2000) views the early career practice as an apprenticeship period in which creatives continue to develop their skillsets and networks to enhance their careers. The question of how to prepare students and identify the skill sets they need is further complicated by the unpredictable development of creative professions, including fashion design (Faerm, 2012), in the context of wider social and economic change.

A limitation of the academic literature on enterprise culture, employability, creative education and creative career development is the dominance of the Global North. Therefore, there is a lack of understanding of how different social and economic contexts and educational frameworks may create different dynamics for creative HE and the CCIs.

Entrepreneurship education in Kenya

Concerning entrepreneurship agendas, Nelson and Johnson (1997: X) note that Kenya was "encouraged to develop a training capacity in entrepreneurship that could lead to the creation of an 'enterprise culture' by the United Nations Development Program (UNDP) and the International Labor Organization (ILO)". Furthermore, Departments of Entrepreneurship Education were opened in most technical training institutions in Kenya (ibid.). Through this initiative (Kenya, 1993: 1) each institution was encouraged to develop a Small Business Centre (SBC) with the mission to "facilitate the development of small and 'Jua Kali' enterprises [small artisan-run manufacturing and service enterprises] and promote an entrepreneurial culture within the institution and the local community". This, according to Nelson and Johnson (1997: X), included the development of a tailored entrepreneurship education curriculum framework covering "(a) entrepreneurship and self-employment, (b) entrepreneurial opportunities, (c) entrepreneurial awareness, (d) entrepreneurial motivation, (e) entrepreneurial competencies, and (d) enterprise management". According to the Policy Framework for Reforming Education and Training for Sustainable Development in Kenya (Republic of Kenya, 2019), entrepreneurial skills and proficiencies are a core component of the education and training systems to be developed.

As in the case of Nigeria (discussed in Chapter 2), the curricula in Kenyan universities and higher education institutions (HEIs) has been criticised for its focus on imparting theoretical knowledge over practical knowledge (Kobia et al., 2017). Research has also shown (Maiyo et al., 2014) that the graduates have very little exposure to the industry, and that the courses are too general, meaning most cannot perform specialised tasks required by the industry. There is also a lack of alignment cited between the industry requirements and what is being taught (Maiyo et al., 2014). This means that employers have to spend another year or more up-skilling graduates so that they can be integrated into the work environment. Particular weaknesses have been identified (Hivos and Equity Bank, 2016) in the following areas: fashion design and management; technical knowledge; entrepreneurship; and finally, product innovation and commercial design. In recognising a disconnect between education and the textiles and apparel industry in particular, there has been a call for training institutions to develop and enhance connections with relevant industries (Nguku, 2012). Further recommendations by Nguku (2012) include the establishment of a stakeholder forum, industry engagement in curriculum development and involvement in departmental expansions.

In exploring fashion design education in the specific context of Kenya, in this chapter we seek to expand our understanding of the role of education and opportunities that it can offer in developing a stronger fashion design sector in Nairobi and beyond.

Kenyan higher education and fashion: an overview

As Nguku (2012) highlights, knowledge and teaching for the fashion sector in Kenya covers a range of disciplines from the more scientific and technological ones (including textile and clothing technology and textile science, but also textile engineering and ginning (textile machinery) engineering). However, in this chapter, we focus specifically on Fashion/ Textile Design and Management. As Nguku (2012: 27) explains, "it basically includes courses that provide students with in-depth knowledge and understanding of the principles of design, fashion and management, together with the skills necessary to succeed as leaders in the vibrant and diverse textile and clothing industry". Nguku also adds that usually these courses "aim to develop creativity, self-reliance and motivation and have a mix of arts and science subjects" (ibid.: 27).

Fashion and textile related courses in Kenya are offered in a number of other universities, private mid-level colleges and TIVETs (Technical Industrial Vocational and Entrepreneurship Training). This structure differs from Western contexts such as the UK where provision is dominated by universities (McRobbie, 2016). The range of courses and providers overall is nevertheless very limited, focusing mainly on textile engineering, fashion design, and garment making. Figure 4.1 maps these different types of educational providers offering fashion-related courses in Kenya. These institutions were identified through the authors' own desktop research and those listed by Nguku (2012), but the list is not exhaustive due to the availability of public information. Furthermore, Table 4.1 outlines the proportion of fashion courses by qualification type and institutional provider.

At the university level, 11 institutions were identified. Admission to these courses is through the Joint Admissions Board (JAB) for government-sponsored students on merit.[1] Universities no longer use admission by portfolio as they are mandated by the government to absorb large numbers of students with varying abilities. There is also a provision for self-sponsored students to enrol in their preferred courses if they were not initially selected. However, this can be problematic in relation to creative courses as it questions the ability of an institution to recruit talented students versus recruiting anyone that can pay for a course.

Aside from university courses, 14 private colleges were mapped, mostly in Nairobi. These providers developed courses in order to meet the ever-increasing demand for tertiary education in Kenya (Sifuna, 2010).

Finally, we identified 27 TIVETs around the country offering certificates, diplomas and artisan courses[2] in garment making and fashion-related courses (Maringa, 2014). These are government institutions under

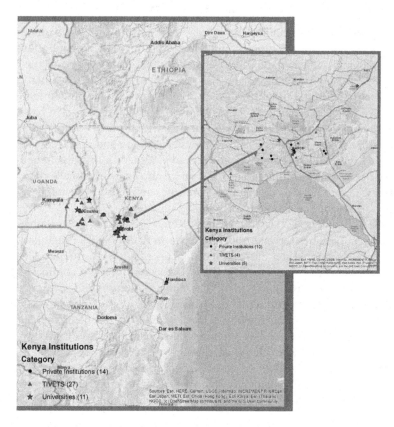

Figure 4.1 Map of Kenyan institutions offering fashion-related courses (data from author's mapping and Nguku, 2012).

the Directorate of Industrial Training (DIT), catering mainly for students who did not attain the marks required for the university courses.[1] These courses are supposed to be more practical in nature, although a report by the DIT shows that technical graduates had little hands-on experience (Maiyo et al., 2014). In general, the TIVETs are spread out across the counties though there is a greater number of institutions situated in Nairobi, the central and western parts of Kenya. Northern Kenya which consists of the largest number of marginalised counties in Kenya (Commission of Revenue Allocation (CRA), 2013) has the smallest number of TIVETs.

In general, the literature suggests that fashion education in Kenya faces some challenges which affect the overall output and quality. These

Table 4.1 Fashion-related courses by qualification and institution type.

Courses*	Total Number	Institutions Offering Fashion-Related Courses		
		Universities	Private Institutions	TIVETS
Artisan Certificate	4	1	0	3
Certificate	40	4	16	22
Diploma	49	7	12	28
BA/BSc	8	7	0	0
MA/BSc	5	5	0	0
PhD in Design	3	3	0	0
		27	28	53

Source: Author's additions to Nguku, 2012.
* The data includes authors' additions, building on the initial mapping of Nguku (2012). We do not include in the table any short courses. The mapping includes a range of courses connected with fashion for example: BA/Certificates/Diplomas in Fashion and Textiles, MAs/PhDs in Design, Diploma/Certificates in Clothing Technology.

include a lack of facilities and capacity to provide adequate training for the students (Kobia et al., 2017); inconsistencies in training standards caused by poor policies (Morris and Levy, 2016) and a lack of continuous investment in the institutions to keep the training up to date with technology and changing trends (Hodges and Link, 2018).

The effects of these challenges are far-reaching. At the moment, the industry is dominated by small enterprises with no more than six employees mainly working on made-to-measure clothing, while large firms employing more than 50 workers constitute 1.5%, and middle scale firms with employees ranging between 11–50 workers constitute 1.4% (Hivos and Equity Bank, 2016). Because of the dearth of skilled individuals suitable for the industry, most of the professionals in the export processing zone (EPZ) where large-scale production occurs, are expatriates. At the same time, the Kenyans work on single basic tasks (Maiyo et al., 2014).

Methodology

The chapter presents the results from fieldwork undertaken as part of funding provided by King's ODA Research Partnership Seed Fund and grown in *Africa Fashion Futures*.[3] The project aimed to map the dynamics of fashion in Africa – specifically through the work of fashion designers – to explore the connections and contradictions between creative and cultural values and the potential for economic development of the creative economy in Africa. The fieldwork focused on two large cities in two anglophone African countries: the capital of Kenya, Nairobi, and the

Figure 4.2 Participants taking part in focus groups discussion in Nairobi on 10th September 2019 (photo: BJ Hracs).

economic capital of Nigeria, Lagos. However, for this chapter we focus specifically on the data collected in Nairobi. We conducted an online survey amongst fashion designers in Nairobi at various stages of their career, collecting 43 responses. Respondents were also invited to attend focus groups to discuss key issues (see Figure 4.2). Out of 43 respondents, 38 accepted the invitation to the focus group discussion. We conducted ten focus groups in total across two groups of 19 fashion designers, each discussing a range of issues from education, to career development, connecting with themes of heritage, networks and supply chains and local and global connections. We also conducted a group interview with three staff members at the University of Nairobi School of Arts and Design. For the purpose of this chapter, we mainly focus on the analysis of the online survey data and the content of the focus group discussion connected with the themes of education and early career development. This data gives us a great insight into the fashion designers actively working in Nairobi and their views on education and knowledge development in the sector.

Nairobi fashion designers: education level and geographies of education

Amongst the group of fashion designers who responded to our survey and took part in the focus groups we identified their education level. The majority of the respondents (32 corresponding to 74%) held a HE undergraduate degree, 5 (12%) held a HE postgraduate degree, only 5 (12%) held other or school-level qualifications and only one person (2%) held no qualification. This highlights how despite the range of providers (see Table 4.1), HE represents the prominent mode of education (86% including undergraduate and postgraduate qualifications) and suggests that in Kenya, HE is a key provider of creative human capital for the fashion design sector, echoing its position in international contexts such as the UK (Comunian and Gilmore, 2016). It also raises questions about the type of education and training provided by HE in relation to the demands and dynamics of local and national industry as explored later in this chapter.

Of the designers with a university degree, all but two had attended a Kenyan institution – one in the USA and one in the UK – and the majority were educated in Nairobi (n = 22, 69%). The University of Nairobi (n = 8) and Kenyatta University (n = 6) were the most commonly attended institutions (Table 4.2). The educational providers and locations represented here partly reflect that this fieldwork was conducted in Nairobi. Those who had a postgraduate qualification (n = 9) represented both Kenyan and international institutions in Italy, London, South Africa and Thailand. One respondent reported an online postgraduate qualification.

Table 4.2 University attended by respondents for their first degree.

University	University Type	Number	University Location
University of Eastern Africa	Private	1	Baraton, Kenya
Daystar University	Private	1	Nairobi, Kenya
Egerton University	Public	1	Njoro, Kenya
Fashion Institute of Technology	Public	1	New York, USA
Kenyatta University	Public	6	Nairobi, Kenya
Machakos University	Public	3	Machakos, Kenya
Maseno University	Public	2	Maseno, Kenya,
Mcensal School of Fashion Design	Private	1	Nairobi, Kenya
Moi University	Public	1	Nairobi, Kenya
Muranga University of Technology	Public	1	Muranga, Kenya
Strathmore University	Private	2	Nairobi, Kenya
The Technical University of Kenya	Public	1	Nairobi, Kenya
University of Bradford, UK	Public	1	Bradford, UK
University of Nairobi	Public	8	Nairobi, Kenya
University of Pretoria	Public	1	South Africa
United States International University-Africa	Private	1	Nairobi, Kenya

Of those designers with a degree, 13 identified that they had a specialist fashion qualification – the most common title was Fashion Design and Marketing (n = 7). However, there were also graduates from non-specialist design programmes (n = 3) and non-creative programmes such as Business/Finance, IT, Media and Communications and other humanities subjects (n = 12 in total). The proportion of graduates from diverse subjects working in the sector brings into question the role of specialised fashion education as an entry route.

It is interesting to reflect on the field of education (for the first degree) of the participants. 17 participants held a Creative degree including Design (4), Media and Comms (1), Fashion Design (3) and Fashion with other minor (Marketing 7 and IT 2); 11 held a non-creative degree including IT (3), Business/ Finance (2), Others (6).

The importance of education and skills for Nairobi fashion designers

The fashion designers who took part in the focus groups articulated that they valued education highly. This was also evidenced in their choice to undertake undergraduate and sometimes postgraduate training locally and internationally. Beyond learning practical skills, they specifically valued the broader perspective that fashion design as an education pathway offered, and the idea that education brings knowledge but also legitimacy to their creative work.

> My education comes like all-round, [...] as a designer I know fabric, how to source, bodyshapes, for the waist, how much time it takes, experience, what is the overall process.
>
> (designer)

Many respondents sought to undertake and invest in their education and considered it a way to distinguish themselves from others but also for the opportunities it offered to engage broadly with the sector. However, others saw how education in itself was not well integrated with policies for the sector. They also discussed the importance of skills for the industry but questioned whether the responsibility to provide this rests only with HE or with a broader platform connecting industry, HE and policy.

> What do we want to achieve as a Kenyan fashion industry? And what direction are we moving in? So that now we tailor our training programmes [...] we're training people here, and the industry is going in this direction. So even by the time you get students out of

the institutions, they're not ready to do what the industry needs [...] there's a need for policy, for us to look at the policies and how it's addressing actual needs of the industry.

(designer and lecturer)

Participants also connected this with the low level of aspiration in the country's policy and industry – aiming at the mass market and not necessarily focusing on the quality of work and skills – which does not necessarily recognise the added value that creativity and the fashion design profession can bring.

The participants with more long-term experience also highlighted the trade-off between education and experience, and the importance of practice. In particular, they discussed the recent tendency for young practitioners to jump into the industry – often using international experience to enter the sector. This was probably driven by increased competition in the sector. However, there was also the argument that this was pushing the quality of the work down and generating a false expectation that "international is better", while younger professionals did not invest as much time into their formal and in-work training.

Why do the people who are training you have to come from Saville Row? [...] We find that that's the gap with the younger generation, when they look at us established designers [...] so they'll come in and intern for three months and not actually take the time it took us to learn, like I worked for three years before I struck out on my own. And so there's this constant perception among designers that international is better.

(designer)

The designers also engaged in a lengthy discussion around the importance of differentiating, while also connecting, the professions of tailor and designer. Designers felt their education and broader creative and business acumen distinguished them from tailors who often would aspire to create labels but without enough knowledge and creative drive. However, there was a recognition that the skills of the tailors they collaborated with – and good working relations and value placed on the quality of tailoring – made an important difference to their business as well as their brand and added value. In this respect, they also highlighted how education could play a role in giving designers better knowledge about tailoring but also in creating partnerships and collaboration between makers and designers as they were all equally important to increase the profile of Kenyan fashion.

Finally, all designers highlighted the importance of being taught entrepreneurship and real-life scenarios in HE settings. They valued working with academics that were also practitioners, that could provide industry briefs and offer them experience beyond skills and techniques to address issues like business planning and real-world strategies for the competitive market.

Conclusions

The chapter has explored the exciting landscape of Kenyan HE provision for fashion and textile courses as well as the recent policy and industry changes in the country.

All the research and policy literature points towards the key role that education can and needs to play in the development of the fashion and textile sector in Kenya. In particular, concerning the use of education as an opportunity to add value rather than developing Kenya as the next world production factory for garments designed elsewhere. In this context, others highlight the importance of connecting curriculum development with "ethical issues, philosophy, innovative technology, and an increasing sensitivity to environmental issues and different cultures" (Marshall (2009) cited in Faerm, 2012: 212).

It is vital for Kenya to maximise the opportunity that some of the international production relocation might create. However, we also acknowledge the importance of skills and knowledge development in the sector. Education, therefore, plays a crucial role in increasing the profile and creative input of Kenya in global fashion markets. In this chapter, beyond reviewing the literature and current education provision, we have sought to present the voice of fashion designers and highlight their own experiences and the value they place on education. In so doing, we have identified that they all acknowledge how education has added value to their work and that education has the potential to add value to the Kenyan fashion sector and production, rather than being a mere producer for fashion designed elsewhere. It also seems essential to connect the opportunity of 'Made in Kenya', and also 'Designed in Kenya' with quality, creativity and the profile of fashion.

Concerning knowledge and skills, the designers discussed the importance of reconciling the skills of tailors with the knowledge of fashion designers. Here they engaged explicitly with the value that high-quality making and tailoring can bring to the 'Made in Kenya' brand in combination with the creative and business skills of designers. Concerning connections between education and industry, the designers discussed the need for universities to expand their work with industry in Kenya.

In particular, engaging directly with designers in order to develop internships and collaborations to bring students up to speed with the challenges of the real world from the start of their studies. Finally, they recognised that skills and training are important beyond HE and that a key challenge for designers – especially for young designers recently out of university – is to find opportunities for ongoing learning, mentoring and networking.

Notes

1 The requirements for a fashion-related degree in Kenya are a mean grade of C+ at secondary level, and a minimum C+ in a combination of subjects including Maths, Languages, Sciences and the Arts.
2 There are a number of different certifications available in Kenya and eligibility depends on the level of education one has completed and the grades achieved. At the lowest level, artisan courses are available to anyone who has completed their primary education, followed by craft certificate courses which are open to holders of secondary level education with a minimum of a D, and diploma courses require a minimum grade of C−. At the highest level, degree courses require a minimum of a C+ (KUCCPS). There are also additional trade tests for artisans where they can gain certification based on specific competencies in their area of expertise (NITA).
3 We acknowledge the support of King's College London ODA (Official Development Assistance) Research Partnership Seed Fund that has led to the award of a *King's Together* Multi and Interdisciplinary Research Scheme award. For more information, see https://www.africa-fashion-futures.org.uk/

References

Ashton D (2016) Creative contexts: Work placement subjectivities for the creative industries. *British Journal of Sociology of Education* 37: 268–287.

Berg A, Hedrich S and Russo B (2015) *East Africa: The next hub for apparel sourcing.* McKinsey & Company.

Boden R and Nedeva M (2010) Employing discourse: Universities and graduate 'employability'. *Journal of Education Policy* 25(1): 37–54.

Brydges T and Hracs BJ (2019) What motivates millennials? How intersectionality shapes the working lives of female entrepreneurs in Canada's fashion industry. *Gender, Place & Culture* 26(4): 510–532.

Caves RE (2000) *Creative industries: Contracts between art and commerce.* Boston: Harvard University Press.

Commission of Revenue Allocation (CRA) (2013) *Survey report on marginalized areas / counties in Kenya.* Available at: https://www.crakenya.org/wp-content/uploads/2013/07/CRA-Revenue-Divison-Among-County-Governments.pdf (accessed 04/06/2020).

Comunian R and Faggian A (2011) Higher education and the creative city. In: Andersson DE, Andersson E and Mellander C (eds) *Handbook of creative cities.* Cheltenham: Edward Elgar Publishing, pp. 187–210.

Comunian R and Gilmore A (2015) *Beyond the creative campus: Reflections on the evolving relationship between higher education and the creative economy.*

Comunian R and Gilmore A (2016) *Higher education and the creative economy: Beyond the campus.* Abingdon: Routledge.

Comunian R, Gilmore A and Jacobi S (2015) Higher education and the creative economy: Creative graduates, knowledge transfer and regional impact debates. *Geography Compass* 9(7): 371–383.

England L (2020) *Crafting professionals in UK higher education: Craft work logics and skills for professional practice.* Unpublished doctoral thesis. London: King's College London.

Faerm S (2012) Towards a future pedagogy: The evolution of fashion design education. *International Journal of Humanities and Social Science* 2(23): 210–219.

Faggian A, Comunian R, Jewell S, et al. (2013) Bohemian graduates in the UK: Disciplines and location determinants of creative careers. *Regional Studies* 47(2): 183–200.

Frenette A and Tepper SJ (2016) What difference does it make? Assessing the effects of arts-based training on career pathways. In: *Higher education and the creative economy.* New York: Routledge, pp. 115–133.

Government of Kenya (2008) *Kenya vision 2030.* Available at: https://kfcb.co.ke/wp-content/uploads/2016/08/vision_2030.pdf (accessed 04/06/2020).

Hivos and Equity Bank (2016) *The Kenyan textile and fashion industry.* Available at: http://www.cottonafrica.com/documents/Fashionomics_report_Kenya_2016.pdf (accessed 06/04/2020).

Hodges NJ and Link AN (2018) Trends in the European textile and apparel industries. In: *Knowledge-intensive entrepreneurship.* Cham: Springer, pp. 29–43.

Houghton N (2016) Six into one: The contradictory art school curriculum and how it came about. *International Journal of Art & Design Education* 35(1): 107–120.

Kamaul PW, Wamutitu JM and Mbugua G (2013) *Employability of fashion and garment making students from youth polytechnics of Kenya.* Vetri Publications, p. 22.

Kenya Ro (1993) *Operational guidelines for small business centers.* Nairobi: Ministry of Research, Technical Training and Technology.

Kobia C, Khoza L, Lee J, et al. (2017) Addressing gaps between textiles and apparel curriculum and the industry in Kenya. International Textiles and Apparel Association(ITAA) Annual Conference Proceedings #74, Florida, 2017. Iowa State University.

Maiyo RC, Abong'o S and Tuigon'g DR (2014) Establishing the training needs of Kenyan university fashion and apparel design graduates. *International Journal of Sciences: Basic and Applied Research* 1(1): 1–10.

Maiyo RC and Imo BE (2012) The Kenyan textile industry in a liberalized economy: An analysis of performance and challenges. *Journal of Emerging Trends in Economics and Management Sciences* 3(1): 111–115.

Maringa M (2014) Proposed interventions for the technical industrial and vocational enterprise training (TIVET) sector in Kenya. *Journal of Technical Education and Training* 6(1): 89-120.

Mastamet-Mason A and Kachieng'a MO (2009) Development of competitive advantage in the apparel industry in Kenya. In: *AFRICON 2009*. IEEE, pp. 1–6.

McKinsey (2019) *The state of fashion 2020*. Available at: https://www.mckinsey.com/~/media/McKinsey/Industries/Retail/Our%20Insights/The%20state%20of%20fashion%202020%20Navigating%20uncertainty/The-State-of-Fashion-2020-final.ashx (accessed 06/04/2020).

McRobbie A (2016) *Be creative: Making a living in the new culture industries.* Cambridge, UK: Polity Press.

Mills C (2011) Enterprise orientations: A framework for making sense of fashion sector start-up. *International Journal of Entrepreneurial Behavior & Research* 17(3): 245–271.

Moore T and Morton J (2017) The myth of job readiness? Written communication, employability, and the 'skills gap' in higher education. *Studies in Higher Education* 42(3): 591–609.

Morris M and Levy B (2016) The limits of cooperation in a divided society: The political economy of South Africa's garment and textile industry. *Towards Employment-Intensive Growth in South Africa.* Cape Town: UCT Press, pp. 327–351.

Nelson RE and Johnson SD (1997) Entrepreneurship education as a strategic approach to economic growth in Kenya. *Journal of Industrial Teacher Education* 35: 7–21.

Nguku E (2012) *Analysis of Textile & Clothing Training Institutions in the East-Southern Africa.* African Cotton and Textile Industries Federation: Nairobi. Available at: www.cottonafrica.com/.../ACTIF%20Report%20of%20Textile.

Olssen M and Peters MA (2005) Neoliberalism, higher education and the knowledge economy: From the free market to knowledge capitalism. *Journal of Education Policy* 20(3): 313–345.

Republic of Kenya (2019) *Sessional paper No. 1 of 2019 on a policy framework for reforming education and training for sustainable development in Kenya.* Available at: http://www.knqa.go.ke/wp-content/uploads/2019/03/Session-Paper-No-1-of-2019.pdf (accessed 06/04/2020).

Sifuna DN (2010) Some reflections on the expansion and quality of higher education in public universities in Kenya. *Research in Post-Compulsory Education* 15(4): 415–425.

Tuigong D, Kipkurgat T and Madara D (2015) Mulberry and silk production in Kenya. *Journal of Textile Science & Engineering* 5(6): 1.

Yorke M (2006) *Employability in higher education: What it is – what it is not.* York: Higher Education Academy.

5 Uganda film and television

Creative skills development and skills gap for the sector

Roberta Comunian and Gershom Kimera

Introduction

There is currently limited academic knowledge and research on the opportunities and challenges faced by the film and television sector in Uganda, nor has it received attention from policymakers, nationally or internationally. Within this broad area of research, this chapter aims to specifically consider the way creative skills in the film and television sector are developed and nurtured, as well as the challenges faced by the current creative workforce concerning skills development and training. The film and television sector, part of the broader creative economy (CE), has attracted plenty of interest from academia and policy in the wider context of Africa both for its cultural and economic development potential (Lobato, 2010; Tomaselli, 2014). However, despite film and television being one of the most dynamic emerging sectors in terms of world exports (Albornoz, 2016), available data and empirical evidence reveal African countries lag behind other regions. The real potential of this sector remains underexploited and knowledge and skills – alongside structural issues – need to be addressed.

Against this backdrop, the case study of Uganda provides valuable insights for a number of reasons; the country has suffered – like many African countries – from a long history of political and civil unrest. This means that only recently new spaces and opportunities for cultural dialogue, development and international engagement have emerged. However, like many other African countries, the cultural heritage, language, traditions and growing youth have put the spotlight on the creative economy and specifically media as an area of growth and development (Strong and Ossei-Owusu, 2014).

The chapter is structured in five parts. Firstly, we provide an overview of the literature and data available in relation to the film and TV sector in Africa and Uganda specifically. Secondly, we provide a more focused analysis of the emergence of the Ugandan film industry: *Kinna-Uganda*. We then detail the methodology used for this study, which is based on qualitative interviews with a range of stakeholders in the Ugandan film and television sector, namely film directors, television station CEO broadcaster managers and producers but also lecturers, university leaders and policymakers.

The study conducted in 2018 also enabled the building of a web-based interactive resource to facilitate knowledge sharing and development in the sector. In the fourth part, we present the analysis of the qualitative interviews articulating our findings around three main themes: skills and higher education (HE) infrastructure, creative workforce training and professional development and broader ecosystem failures. We conclude the chapter by reflecting on some of the initial steps taken in policy and on the importance of international cooperation for future development, specifically in relation to skills and knowledge. It suggests a window of opportunity exists for the researcher and educational institutions to play a role in influencing policies and practices in the Ugandan creative and cultural industries (CCIs).

Researching film and television in Africa and Uganda

There is currently limited research and knowledge about the African film and television industry in many African countries because the sector is poorly researched, supported and understood (Haynes, 2010). A notable exception which has attracted the global attention of the studios and researchers is Nigeria's film industry popularly known as 'Nollywood'. The success story of Nollywood, now the second biggest film producer per annum in volume after India (UNESCO, 2009) is well documented in academia (Lobato, 2010; Tomaselli, 2014). Moreover, it has been used as a flagship case by international bodies such as UNESCO to argue for the potential of creative economies in the economic development of Africa.

However, Nollywood remains a very isolated case in Africa and less than 20 countries (out of 54) even make it into the UNESCO Statistical dataset for film features (Table 5.1).

Looking at other research on the film and television sector across Africa and beyond, we can recognise some common themes: the role of skills and knowledge and the struggle for their acquisition (Grugulis and Stoyanova, 2009); the importance of support and investment (Collins and Snowball, 2015) and the connection between local and international demand on quality and innovation (Barnard and Tuomi, 2008). Research from South Africa (Collins and Snowball, 2015) considers the important

Table 5.1 Dataset of feature films. Total number of national feature films produced across African countries.

	Year						
	2011	*2012*	*2013*	*2014*	*2015*	*2016*	*2017*
Country*							
Algeria	—	—	—	—	—	21	12
Angola	—	—	—	—	—	6	4
Burkina Faso	—	18	16	24	5	—	—
Burundi	—	—	—	7	1	14	5
Egypt	28	25	33	42	34	38	—
Eritrea	—	41	39	35	28	15	11
Gabon	10	10	9	—	—	—	—
Madagascar	—	—	—	51	36	14	12
Mauritius	1	—	—	18	9	17	9
Morocco	24	22	22	17	18	30	37
Mozambique	—	—	—	11	25	23	31
Niger	6	—	—	—	—	—	—
Nigeria	997	—	—	—	—	—	—
Senegal	5	2	3	3	3	5	2
South Africa	22	19	25	23	22	28	23
South Sudan	—	—	—	—	43	—	—
Togo	—	18	23	16	19	—	3
Tunisia	11	8	8	—	11	—	—

Source: UNESCO, 2019: extracted on 20 Jan 2020 from June 2019 Update from UIS.Stat.
* We extracted data for all African countries but only reported the countries where data were available for at least one of the years included in the analysis.

impact that the film and television sector can have more broadly – including pre- and post-production activities – as well as the importance of attracting foreign companies to film and produce in African countries. In order to attract these kinds of investments, subsidies and policy support are needed (ibid.).

In Uganda's case, limited data is available on *Kinna-Uganda (K-U)*, which is not included in the UNESCO statistical count (see Table 5.1) despite recent attention being placed on the country production after Semwogerere's groundbreaking first commercial feature *Feeling Struggle* (2005) and others that continue to be produced (see Table 5.2).

Uganda is one of the poorest countries in the world. According to Uganda poverty reduction strategy paper progress report (IMF, 2014), per capita income was $646 with 19.7% of the population living below the poverty line. Therefore, benchmarking K-U quality and work with that of international case studies in the Global North or even the Global South would be inappropriate. However, it is important to consider

Table 5.2 Timeline for the main films produced under the umbrella of Kinna-Uganda.

Film Director(SURNAME, name)	Title	Year	Awards/Recognitions
MISANVU, Faustin J	*It's Not Easy*	1991	Prix Futura – Berlin. National Council on Family Relations – The New York Festival
SSEMWOGERERE, Ashraf	*London Shock*	2000	WBS Televisom Uganda
SSEMWOGERERE, Ashraf	*Feelings Struggle*	2005	First commercial feature Kinna-Uganda. Bukedde Tv
SSEMWOGERERE, Ashraf	*Ssuubi (Hope)*	2008– 2014	
NABWANA, Isaac Godfrey Geoffrey	*Who Killed Captain Alex?*	2010	First "Kinna -Uganda" Action movie
MUGERWA, Abbey	*Save the Mothers World Toilet Day Circumcision*	2014	Sundance Film Festival
MUGERWA, Daniel	*RAIN*	2017	Best women's rights film – London Eye Film Network Ltd.
SSOZI, Moses	*11th July Ekikangabwa*	2018	N/A
SSEMWOGERERE, Ashraf	*Crazy Vivian Fear of Death*	2019 2019	N/A

how *Kinna-Uganda* has made international headlines and how this offers opportunities for further research and potential development for the local film and television sector (Slavkovic, 2015).

Historically, as highlighted by Rasmussen (2010), *Kinna-Uganda* is the term used to denote the film production developed in Uganda after the collapse of the totalitarian regime of Idi Amin in 1979. This means the development of a national Ugandan film production, which is financially supported by Ugandan funds (either personal or business entity) and directed by a Ugandan artist/film director. For purposes of this study, we refer to this as the Ugandan film and television media production, which includes films and television programmes produced and financed by Ugandans in Uganda.

As summarised in Table 5.2, there have been a limited number of K-U productions with some gaining international recognition. Some of the film directors have been interviewed as part of this research project, however, it is clear that the Ugandan industry is still in its infancy. A few productions had taken place before 2005, however at the time there were no critics to identify the rise of *Kinna-Uganda* until Ashraf Semwogerere's 2005 feature, *Feelings Struggle*, was referred to as Uganda's first commercial feature *film*. Nabwana's (2010) *Who Killed Captain Alex?* seems to be the first known Ugandan proper action feature film (Venema, 2015). Some international blockbusters movies – although not Uganda funded or directed – such as *Last King of Scotland* (directed by Kevin Macdonald) or *Mississippi Masala* (directed by Mira Nair) took inspiration from Ugandan stories and placed a spotlight on the country's landscapes and traditions without bringing new development.

The K-U films and works in Table 5.2 and others not included in this study directed attention towards Uganda's film industry, while also raising questions about its workings and future directions. Kamukama (2012) critically acknowledges that in Uganda there is a lack of opportunity for recognition of Ugandan and in general African films, with awards taking place irregularly due to financial constraints. She argues that the Uganda film industry has suffered 'stillbirth' as it "has failed to harness the advantage and steer the local film industry out of oblivion. Uganda's film industry [...] has persistently remained stunted even as the number of players in the industry grows by the day" (Kamukama, 2012). To foster collaboration and recognition, a group of theatre performing actors, actresses and musicians in Uganda established the Uganda Film Network (UFN). The remit of the organisation – although operating with very limited resource and funding – was to nurture a Ugandan "infant film industry" especially censorship of films, seeking sponsorship, research and rewarding filmmakers.

Kamukama (2012) highlights the lack of finance and resources of *Kinna-Uganda* as well as the lack of educational infrastructure, given that only Kampala University has a fully-fledged film department. While she points to a potentially large pool of talent, with over 900 UFN-accredited filmmakers, she nevertheless questions where their films are.

With respect to policy, the Uganda Communications Commission (UCC) is the official government regulatory body of the communications (including film and television) sector in Uganda. Although owned by the government, it acts independently. Beyond responsibilities in licensing, regulation and communications infrastructure development, the UCC has been behind the development of the Uganda Film Festival (UFF). The UFF was established in 2013 to promote the local film industry both domestically and internationally, and to bring industry stakeholders together.

From this broad overview, it appears that the development of *Kinna-Uganda* and its potential for the future is linked to the possibility for new or emerging filmmakers to produce more films. However, the infrastructure for creative skills in Uganda is very scarce and this is where our research aims to focus and contribute. Firstly, by mapping what is available and secondly by thinking about the broader question of how the skills gap could be filled and how Ugandan film and television media production industry could be professionalised.

Research journey and methodology

This research began with a desire to reflect on the knowledge and skills development in the Ugandan film and television media production sector. One of the authors was a former practitioner in the Ugandan industry without any formal training in the practice as there were hardly any institutions offering it in the country during the 1990s and early 2000s. The research trajectory pointed towards the UK higher education institutions (HEIs) for further training. This speaks to a broader concern around the skills and knowledge required in the film and television industry as a discipline and how this could be transferred or enhanced in the context of the Ugandan film and television media production industry.

From the very beginning it emerged that there are very few HEIs offering dedicated training in film and television or media production as an independent program in Uganda; even those institutions offering media courses such as mass communication and journalism only include a shallow component of video, film production and television presentation. The exception is Kampala University which has a film department and offers courses up to diploma level. This situation, coupled with limited scholarly literature, steered the project towards two key research questions: (1) What is the role of skills, knowledge and training in the development of Kinna-Uganda? (2) What are the challenges and barriers to the professionalisation of the Ugandan film and television media production industry?

After an extensive literature review on skills in the film and television sector internationally and specifically focused on Africa (Collins and Snowball, 2015), the authors reflected on the importance of collecting data and adopting an ethnographic approach. It was expected that this would provide the most insight for our research questions and so builds on ethnography of filmmaking (Henley, 1998). The research was conducted between 2017 and 2018 and the findings were presented as an online, web-based interactive resource.[1] The methodology involved two main data collection methods: participant observation and qualitative, semi-structured, in-depth interviews. In reference to the participant observation (Musante and DeWalt, 2010), we adopted a 'moderate' type of participant observation trying to maintain a balance between being an 'insider' and an 'outsider' (Spradley, 2016). This required a systematic, purposeful and selective way of listening, recording and watching of practitioners as they go about their normal filming on four different locations in Kampala (see Figure 5.1 and 5.2).

Occasionally, they would be informally asked a few questions regarding their practice. This was helpful because work practices were exposed that could not have been accurately described within qualitative

Figure 5.1 Filmmaker Moses Ssozi of MN Films Africa discussing with members of his crew (photo: G Kimera).

Figure 5.2 Filmmaker Abbey Mugerwa of Storyline Pictures during filming activities (photo: G Kimera).

interviews. Observation also focused on issues with health and safety for entire crew, cast and the public.

In relation to the interviews, the project involved and engaged with a range of practitioners, television broadcasters, educators, filmmakers as well as key stakeholders in K-U industry. These were centred on understanding their individual journeys and trajectories for skills development but also identified gaps and opportunities for the future development of the Ugandan film and television production sector. The interviews discussed a range of topics from the sector's historical background and their own educational and professional background to their view on the sector, the quality of productions, and the challenges faced by the industry. The research also sought to investigate possible solutions and recommendations for professionalising the industry.

Although not the focus of this chapter, grounded in film studies research methods, documentary[2] filmmaking was also used not only as a tool for collecting data at certain phases but as a form of 'scholarly publication' in its own right. Therefore, most of the interviews undertaken were also documented in video format and as such, another output of the research became a web-based interactive documentary to represent, interpret, engage and publish this art-informed visually researched work. While the documentary and project involved a large sample of participants, including participants on the web platform, for the purpose of this chapter we focus on the core 14 research interviews.[3] A description of the sample is provided in Table 5.3. While the project was focused on training institutions and the creative skills needs, it clearly emerged in the interviews that these could not be addressed in isolation and that in order to understand them it was important to consider a range of stakeholders to identify the current challenges.

The study had of course a range of limitations, especially in consideration of the small sample. However, it offers some initial insights into the development of the Ugandan film and television sector that will hopefully be taken forward by further research.

Discussion: understanding skills, knowledge and challenges of Kinna-Uganda

Creative skills development in Uganda: training and education

In Uganda, the number of HEIs that offer courses in film production is very limited. Kampala University has a reserved department for film and television. Outside of this and a few other smaller institutions around Kampala, according to our interviewee, there are no other places where aspiring filmmakers can get hands-on knowledge, "Not even at the

Table 5.3 Interview research sample, including qualification, position and years of experience in the sector.

Uganda Film & Television Industry Sector	N.	Qualification Level	Sex	Initials	Position	Years of Experience
Lecturers/HE	1	Degree and above	M	G ASB	Senior Lecturer	15<
	2	Univ. degree and above	F	SK	Dept. Head	10<
	3	Degree and above	F	JN	Senior Lecturer	7<
	4	Degree and above	M	NB	Senior Lecturer	5<
	5	Degree and above	M	FO	Senior Lecturer	10<
Production Practitioners and Managers	6	Degree and above	M	JS	Production Manager	15<
	7	Degree	M	GS	Production Manager	21<
	8	Degree and above	M	FJM	Producer/Director	30<
Independent Film Directors	9	Self-taught	M	AM	Manager	10<
	10	Degree	M	AS	Producer/ Director	15<
Broadcasters	11	Degree and above	M	SK	Senior Presenter	5<
	12	Degree and above	M	TM	Author & Broadcaster	15<
	13	Degree	M	GS	Production Manager	15<
Regulators	14	Univ. degree and above	F	RK	Manager Content Generation	5<
	15	Degree and above	M	PM	Manager Content Regulation	5<

prestigious Makerere University" (AS, Film Director). Others, like FJM, film and television producer, also reflected on the lack of training opportunities: "we're lacking dedicated film and television professional training and very few people go abroad for professional or specialised professional training".

Many highlighted that this is a historical legacy of the slow development of the sector in Uganda following the collapse of the totalitarian regime of Amin in 1979. In fact, a senior media consultant (author and broadcaster for Television and Radio) TM, explained "we don't have so many people who have trained in film [...] the training institutions lack facilities [...] and lack lecturers". Therefore, the lack of provision is considered by many of the participants as a structural and institutional gap in the development of Ugandan film and television. Beyond this, the quality of training provided was also often questioned by practitioners.

> there are a number of academies / institutions where they commercially recruit students and train them in film production, but they are not specialised film institutions. They also do a number of other vocational trainings [...] we have many young people finishing education that have a problem finding what to do.
>
> (FJM, Film and Television Practitioner)

HE providers must keep up both with changing technologies – that might make training with cameras more affordable – and the growing demand for this area of study. As two practitioners involved in film and television training at the university level highlighted, there has been a shift in the provision with a growing interest among Uganda's youth in this sector of study and work:

> when I came here the training was basically theory based, they would draw a picture of a camera on the blackboard [...] then they move on to acquiring one camera [...] as people got more and more interested in the industry the enrolment rocketed. Now we have classes of 180 students.
>
> (GS, Senior Lecturer)

Therefore, even though the cost of technology is decreasing and becoming more affordable, the provision remains a challenge: "we have a media lab studio but there is hardly any time for practice (close to 400 students)" (ibid.).

Due to the lack of infrastructure and investment in HE-level training, many study abroad, which has characterised the specialisation of film and television producers in Uganda for the last 20 years and endures: "They go abroad and just have a course component about production where they do camera work and what have you. Then they come back" (MJF, film and television practitioner). While international training can provide a positive input, it raises questions of access (who can afford to train abroad) and the diversity of voices and stories of the sector.

The creative workforce in film and television in Uganda: skills and professional practice

In our research, the lack of opportunities is not limited to HE but also lies in career and further professional development. As GS, an older film director and producer, highlights when he started working there was only one broadcaster in 1985: "Only a few people knew something to do with TV production. It was only a few people that had been given a job in TV that had a chance to be taken abroad to train". Accordingly, for a long time it was only access to a career in the sector that could provide an opportunity for specialised training (abroad). Despite the restrictions and limitations of relying on the possibility to train on the job to develop a career, the older generation were able to benefit from a broadcasting infrastructure and a sector which was not yet suffering due to global competition. This was also confirmed by a senior lecturer and former practitioner who highlighted that while the opportunities in the 1980s were very limited, because of the concentration of resources on a few institutions, "core staff would join untrained, but then they would be trained on the job and they would also be taken abroad for training because there was no television/film training school here" (GASB, Senior Lecturer).

While the general situation for creative workforce training has not changed much, the actual quality and investment in on-the-job training has reduced due to the growing competition between providers alongside the broader appeal of film and television careers among the younger generation. "Private stations came up, they are more for commercial purposes, economic benefits. So one of the things to cut costs was that they wouldn't take people for training" (GASB, Senior Lecturer).

In fact, many of the interviewees highlighted the lack of skills as a feature of the industry per se and that moving across tasks and a subsequent lack of specialisation was also prevalent across the sector.

> We have people who are not professionally specialised, people who are not professional scriptwriters [...] people who have no idea of

proper production and professional directing [...] they pick up a few actors here and there, and find somebody who can record footage.

(FJM, Film & Television Practitioner)

Most of the practitioners had a stage acting background, as observed by senior media consultant (author and broadcaster for Television and Radio) TM:

the local film industry's main challenge has persistently lain in the failure to distinguish stage acting from screen acting. [...] The recent decline in theatre entries has forced many dramatists to drag their amateur stage skills to screen.

This lack of specialisation and the weight of having to develop one's career on individual resources is a common issue for creative workers across the world (Jones and DeFillippi, 1996; Ibert and Schmidt, 2012) but is exacerbated in Uganda by the general lack of opportunities for knowledge access and specialised education. For some, YouTube becomes the only accessible source of training:

I started as a cameraman but I had more passion in editing [...]. But I have been learning through tutorials online, most of my [learning] experience has been online via YouTube.

(AM, Practitioner)

The lack of investment in training and skills has substantial implications not only for the sector but also for *Kinna-Uganda* as an ecosystem (discussed further in the next section), with limited potential for growth. GS, (Uganda Broadcasting Corporation (UBC) production manager) broadcaster, highlights that historically *Kinna-Uganda* started when video cameras became cheap and accessible to those who were enthusiastic about making films: "People started making very poor films because they had no skills [...]. They never knew about the technology, they did not take care of sound" (GS, broadcaster). However, while better technologies became more readily available, the country saw increasing global competition, with new productions coming into the country from all over the world.

with this explosion [of technologies] also came a defiance towards basic production values in the name of innovation, in the name of what the computer can give you [...]. People thinking "as long as I can cut and paste a production together".

(GASB, Senior Lecture)

Some respondents identified a sort of age gap connected with ways of working and quality, also linked to this technological – rather than content-based – focus:

> like the way young people do things, is not the way we used to. I'd say what has really improved is picture quality [...]. But when it comes to actual content, TV stations have not done enough in terms of bringing out what you would call content.
>
> (JS, Manager/Producer TV Station)

Many highlighted a lack of depth in the stories and content filmed and presented. This limited attention on quality and content is also connected to the growing financial pressure felt by the sector: "some might have good cameras but they are rushing to get, I think, money out of their production, they don't give it enough time to do something good" (AM Practitioner).

In a vicious cycle, this renders productions even less attractive to local broadcasters due to a lack of viewer interest, which subsequently decreases the market for the local productions further. It also reconnects with the lack of education provision when *Kinna-Uganda* competes internationally as "the people who give you marks are those who are professionals" (TM, author and broadcaster for Television and Radio) and are part of a highly specialised technical and cultural global network.

Ecosystem failures: law, markets and distribution challenges

Of course, for many respondents, the challenges connected to the quality and opportunities for training and skills for creatives cannot be understood in isolation but need to be contextualised within a creative ecosystem with multiple connected weaknesses and structural failures. One of the main challenges of the system is linked to piracy and copyright practices that do not protect content producers and value creation.

> Of course the copyright is causing a lot of headache. There is a new law but it is barely enforceable [...] even the law enforcement officers, the justice law [...] does not properly comprehend the meaning of copyright.
>
> (MJF, Producer/Director)

Therefore, piracy needs to be also situated within an industry that remains largely informal and unprofessional. The lack of knowledge and practices concerning how the film sector works and how it can be financed are also part of the bigger picture (see Chapter 8 in this book). In this ecosystem, many specifically pointed to the role played by VJs[4] as undermining the foundation of the system and the possibility to grow future audiences. Downloaded pirated films of Hollywood quality, with multimillion-dollar production costs, are edited with sound, jokes and commentary additions in the local language (Luganda), which audiences understand and enjoy. Such films are commonly watched in local video halls.

> You can see the "bibanda" (the makeshift video halls) all over the country and the culture of people attending modern cinemas is also very low. You find that most of the films are exhibited in the illegal poorly structured bibanda (Video halls).
>
> (PM regulator)

This is connected to a lack of understanding and investment in the film and television media production sector and its traditional business models, but also to a lack of academic attention towards the different dynamics of video (vs. film) production in many African countries (Haynes, 2010). AS, a film director, highlights:

> in Uganda when we produce we start with the end point, e.g. you produce, you start selling the DVD on the launch, which is not the case with Hollywood, for example [...] but for us we start with the end thus we get little.

Therefore, the sector is not able to build a model to fund itself. Most practitioners cannot afford to contract distribution companies; neither can they afford to premier their films. As soon as they finish making a film, they either sell DVDs for quick money or put them on YouTube.

A further disconnect in the ecosystem concerns the ability of local producers to connect with a local or national broadcaster. Another producer/manager highlights that the proliferation of TV stations has brought up new talent but this has not led to a growth of the industry: "no television station is capable of paying for local content, it is very expensive, so film makers are funding their productions. There are over 30 stations but only about two stations are buying local content" (GS, UBC Production Manager). The impact of technology in this sense has not helped producers but created further competition.

Furthermore, the local infrastructure and skills are not competitive enough with the international content coming into the country. As AS,

ProducerDirector, summarises "we are getting eaten up by foreign content, by a very big % because it is cheap and has high quality". The local productions – even for local drama – cost five times more than the imported ones.

Local policies by the UCC have put forward proposals for a "local content development fund". However, the same stations that should support this local content find it challenging:

"we imposed a quota on television stations they have to air 70% local content. The pay-TV stations said by the nature of their programming, it is not possible for them to comply" (RK, Manager Content regulation at UCC). These interventions remain a work in progress and the authorities have not yet approved the proposal.

However, for other respondents, like JS, Manager/Producer TV Station, attention should not only be directed to production costs and quality, but also to audiences. He asked, "why would some people prefer watching Filipinos to local Ugandan drama?". The more significant challenge is the education of audiences and the value they get from the representation of Ugandan culture and content. The problem, he continues, is connected with a whole generation of Uganda film audiences who have grown up with the common practice of VJs[3] re-worked films for very cheap and are not willing to pay more for local content.

Conclusions and future perspectives

This chapter has explored the role of skills in film and television in Uganda. The findings highlight that Uganda still requires investment in creative skills – both within the context of formal HE and concerning in-house and on-the-job training. As one of the interviewees summarised, the lack of development and growth of the film industry is "a very long story but at the heart of it is an absence of (a) training (b) professionalism (c) enabling environment to be able to produce and market and distribution of films" (MJF, Producer/Director).

One might think that the education and skills gap could be addressed simply by some international academic partnership or more competitive media businesses. However, we found that this was not only the outcome of a poor infrastructure but the outcome of a long-term under-valuing and disinvestment in the broader ecosystem for creative film and television development. Nonetheless, many reflected on the fact that the film industry in Uganda is still in the development stage. It is still growing and looking back at where it started from – not so long ago – there is scope for further growth.

In fact, it has become apparent in the development of our discussion that more structural interventions are needed which indirectly might serve to drive towards better skills and better skills provision. In order to improve quality however, respondents reflected on the importance of giving creatives time to work on their stories but also time to learn and access to professionals to train them. Some practitioners reported on the positive input of new players coming in and making a difference. For example, they mentioned the work in film promotion done by organisations like Maisha film labs, a non-profit training initiative for emerging East African filmmakers, that provides intensive training in screenwriting, directing and producing. The role of international partnerships is also important for others, although with scope for further sector-specific collaboration: "for photography Kenyans and South Africans have been here and done some workshops but for film [skills] not, I have not seen any" (AM, Practitioner).

For another Producer/Director (MJF) it was important to create more guilds and groups to bring together creative producers and workers to better define the value of their work and skills. It was acknowledged that the type of training and development needs to match a job title but also enable the protection of producers' or workers' rights across the sector. Another step – lauded by one of the interviewees – was the UCC's decision to organise the UFF,

> so people submit their work and it is subjected to rigorous evaluation. Winners are rewarded for the best production that corresponds to those values […]. So the producers […] have learnt the values of good production values and so have the audience.
>
> (GASB Senior Lecturer)

Again, these interventions do not directly address the challenge of training and skills, but promote more broadly an environment in which those skills might be valued. One producer told us that as a member of UFF he had been overwhelmed by the work presented in 2017: "over 120 films including Docs and feature, I can see quite an improvement on quality" (GS, Producer/Manager).

Policy interventions from the UCC, like the UFF, are a step in the right direction, especially with training workshops bringing in experts and filmmakers from around the world to provide free training and the showcasing of Ugandan content. These interventions, however, also need to continue to engage with the structural challenges that exist in the wider ecosystem.

Notes

1 For more information visit https://www.ugandafilmskill.com.
2 Ethics approval for the entire research project was obtained from the University of Portsmouth (UK).
3 The authors would like to thank all participants and other stakeholders in the Ugandan film industry, as well as family and friends, that supported the project.
4 VJs is short for video jokers who take mainstream productions and narrate them in the local language, adding their own commentary (see Venema, 2015 for more details).

References

Albornoz LA (2016) *Diversity and the film industry: An analysis of the 2014 UIS survey on feature film statistics.* UNESCO Institute for Statistics.

Barnard H and Tuomi K (2008) How demand sophistication (de-)limits economic upgrading: Comparing the film industries of South Africa and Nigeria (Nollywood). *Industry and Innovation* 15(6): 647–668.

Collins A and Snowball J (2015) Transformation, job creation and subsidies to creative industries: The case of South Africa's film and television sector. *International Journal of Cultural Policy* 21(1): 41–59.

Grugulis I and Stoyanova D (2009) 'I don't know where you learn them': Skills in film and TV. In: *Creative labour: Working in the creative industries*, pp. 135–155.

Haynes J (2010) A literature review: Nigerian and Ghanaian videos. *Journal of African Cultural Studies* 22(1): 105–120.

Henley P (1998) Film-making and ethnographic research. In: *Image-based research: A sourcebook for qualitative researchers*, pp. 42–59.

Ibert O and Schmidt S (2012) Acting on multiple stages: How musical actors construct their labour-market vulnerability and resilience. *Raumforschung und Raumordnung Spatial Research and Planning* 70(4): 349–361.

IMF (2014) *Uganda poverty reduction strategy paper – Progress report.* Available at: https://www.imf.org/external/pubs/ft/scr/2014/cr14354.pdf (accessed 23/05/2020).

Jones C and DeFillippi RJ (1996) Back to the future in film: Combining industry and self-knowledge to meet the career challenges of the 21st century. *Academy of Management Perspectives* 10(4): 89–103.

Kamukama P (2012) *Ugandan films suffer stillbirth.* Available at: observer.ug/index.php?option=com_content&view=article&id=16666:ugandan-films-suffer-stillbirth&catid=42:sizzling-entertainment&Itemid=74 (accessed 19/02/2020).

Lobato R (2010) Creative industries and informal economies: Lessons from Nollywood. *International Journal of Cultural Studies* 13(4): 337–354.

Musante K and DeWalt BR (2010) *Participant observation: A guide for fieldworkers.* Rowman Altamira: Plymouth, UK.

Rasmussen KA (2010) *Kinna-Uganda: A review of Uganda's national cinema.* Available at: https://scholarworks.sjsu.edu/etd_theses/3892.

Slavkovic M (2015) Filmmaking in East Africa: Focus on Kenya, Tanzania, and Uganda. In: *Small cinemas in global markets: Genre, identities, narratives*, pp. 189–214.

Spradley JP (2016) *Participant observation*. Long Grove: Waveland Press.

Strong K and Ossei-Owusu S (2014) Naija boy mixi: Afroexploitation and the new media creative economies of cosmopolitan African youth. *Journal of African Cultural studies* 26(2): 189–205.

Tomaselli KG (2014) Nollywood production, distribution and reception. *Journal of African Cinemas* 6(1): 11–19.

UNESCO (2019) UNESCO Institute for Statistics (UIS): Features film dataset. In: Statistics UIf (ed.).

UNESCO P (2009) *Nollywood rivals bollywood in film/video production*. UNESCO Institute for Statistics.

Venema V (2015) *Uganda's Tarantino and his $200 action movies*. Available at: https://www.bbc.com/news/magazine-32531558 (accessed 23/05/2020).

Who Killed Captain Alex? (2010) Directed by Issac Nabwana. Uganda: Nabwana IGG and Alan Ssali Hofmanis.

PART 2

The role of policy for creative economies

6 Importance of arts and culture in community development in Nigeria

The place of the Councils for Arts and Culture

Duro Oni, Cornelius Onyekaba and Shaibu Husseini

Introduction: culture for national development

The term culture has been subjected to many definitions because culture means different things to different people. Raymond Williams, the British cultural critic, famously asserted that "culture is one of the two or three most complicated words in the English language" (Williams, 1976: 87). As Williams (1976) further explained, culture represents a totality of people's way of life including materials, institutional and philosophical orientation. This may be why Archer (as cited in Wilson et al., 2020: 22) observes that culture, on the one hand, engulfs and orchestrates the entire social structure and on the other, is charged only with providing an ideational representation of the structure.

Similarly, Wilson (2020) argues that culture can best be understood as involving both the systems we collectively put in place for recognising values and our experiencing values for ourselves. Udoh (2003) provides another perspective when he defined culture as representing a shared understanding of norms, rules and laws that govern and control the behaviour and beliefs of a group of people. Bello (as cited in Alhamdu, 2008: 56) sees culture as an aggregate of human behaviours which includes elements in man's natural endowment that he has acquired from his group by conscious learning or on somewhat different levels, by a conditioning process, technique of various kinds, social and other institutions, belief and patterned modes of conduct.

The 1988 Cultural Policy of Nigeria defines culture as

> the totality of the way of life evolved by a people in their attempts to meet the challenge of living in their environment, which gives order

and meaning to their social, political, economic, aesthetic and religious norms and modes of organisation thus distinguishing a people from their neighbours.

(CPN, 1988: 3)

The policy further enumerates the characteristics of culture to comprise a *material aspect* which has to do with artefacts in its broadest form (including tools, clothing, food, medicine, utensils and so on); the *institutional* (including political, social, legal and economic structures erected to help achieve material and spiritual objectives); the *philosophical* which is concerned with ideas, beliefs and values; and the *creative* aspect which is concerned with people's oral or written literature as well as their visual and performing arts which help to mould other aspects of culture.

However, Uyah (2006) argues that culture should no longer be viewed as a dimension but as the very fabric of society in its global relationship with development. In other words, culture embraces all aspects of a people's way of life and it is comprised of the social, political, economic, technological and artistic variables that aid development and make life easier and better in any given society. Furthermore, Ayakoroma (2015) posits that culture should rightfully embody the attitudes of people towards their traditional values in the future when faced with the demands of modern technology, which is an essential factor of development. Kimanuka (2016) stresses the importance of culture to the socio-political and economic development of a given society when he opined that culture is one of the main pillars of development and sustenance of communities, and as such no society can progress in its absence. According to Kimanuka (2016), traditional celebrations are some of the core aspects of any culture. Whether it is a wedding, a harvest or national observance, our celebrations are woven tightly into our overall cultural identity. Celebrating our traditions offers an excellent opportunity for intercultural exchange and understanding. Kimanuka (2016) further asserts that it is these undertakings that contribute to an increase in the intellectual potential with the attendant positive implication of building a conscious, open, tolerant and progressive society.

By extension, the term 'development' often connotes growth and expansion. However, it is simply the act of advancement, growth or change from one stage to another marked by considerable progress (Aig-Imoukhuede, 2006). According to Akogun (2003), development means some sort of social change, growing complexity and increased capacity to carry out more complicated tasks and functions. In the context of this chapter, development simply implies change or improvement in the wellbeing of the citizens of a given society including factors that influence a community and change the quality of life of citizens through participation in cultural activities. This has the implication of improving citizens' career, social, financial, physical and community wellbeing.

As such, it is evident that there is a relationship between culture and development. Nigerian cultural policy analyst Olu Obafemi (2005: 9) captures this relationship and the important role of culture in community development writing that "culture is fundamental to human existence and human civilisation, embodying in its dynamism, the totality of people's response to the challenges of life and living in any given environment". For Obafemi, the intrinsic value of culture in society means it is a prerequisite consideration for any development. In agreement, Ayakoroma (2015) and Jegede (2015) note that culture can be used as a reflection of standards attained in a society at a given point in time.

In Nigeria, the important role that culture plays in national development is evidenced in the establishment of structures that help to promote both local and international creative economies, such as the State Council for Arts and Culture (SCAC) and the National Council for Arts and Culture (NCAC). Their primary responsibility is to promote and foster an appreciation, revival and development of Nigerian arts and culture and to facilitate improvement in the socio-economic life of the people at the local, state and national level. This paper examines the role of culture in community development through the activities of SCAC and NCAC. The chapter presents a review of Nigerian cultural policy, informed by historical and critical policy approaches (see Scullion and Garcia 2005 for a review of cultural policy methods). Moreover, the chapter benefitted from the insights of three key experts' interviews.[1]

Nigeria and cultural development

The central role of culture in the development process led several countries to design and introduce policies, programmes and actions on how culture should be managed for the benefit of the citizens especially those at a grassroots level. As a country, Nigeria was amongst the few countries in sub-Saharan Africa that identified and embraced culture as a veritable instrument for national development (Akogun, 2003). According to Bello (as cited in Alhamdu, 2008: 20), there was an increasing awareness amongst Nigeria's political authority in the mid 1970s that asserting Nigeria's cultural identity could be a means of bringing about positive changes in their national outlook as well as in establishing greater confidence in their national values and aspirations. There was indeed a conscious effort by the then Military government, particularly after the Nigerian civil war (1967–1970) to use culture as an instrument for promoting national unity and integration (Alhamdu, 2008). Thus in 1972, the then Military government created a Department of Culture from what used to be a Cultural Division within the Ministry of Information. The government also established the NCAC in 1975 as an autonomous agency of the Ministry of Information (Asiwaju, 1990). The defunct Cultural Division superintended the hosting of the National Festival of Arts and Culture, which was first held in 1970 in Lagos and subsequently in 1971 in Ibadan and in 1972 in Kaduna, Nigeria. Essentially, the festivals were used to promote "unity in diversity", a slogan that resonated in subsequent festivals (Figure 6.1).

Undoubtedly, Nigeria witnessed a sort of cultural renaissance at Independence. Arinze (2001) noted that there was a clamour to go back to the past and for culture to be used as a platform for national integration and development. Indeed, the realisation that culture was the *sine qua non* for national development led to the establishment of more State Councils responsible for arts and culture and several other cultural institutions including the National Gallery of Arts (NGA) and the National Commission for Museum and Monuments (NCMM), all in a bid to harness the potentials of arts and culture for national development.

However, cultural trends in the 1970s heightened with Nigeria's hosting of the 2nd World Black Festival of Arts and Culture (FESTAC) held in Lagos and Kaduna state, respectively. The success of FESTAC 77 provided the impetus for the speedy development of Nigeria's culture both at the state and national levels. State governments that hitherto did not establish SCACs saw the need to set up a council responsible for arts and cultural matters over the year.

Similarly, the federal government established more cultural institutions including the Centre for Black and African Arts and Civilisation (CBAAC), the institutional body and repository agency that emerged from FESTAC 77 to oversee future festivals, activities and documents that emanated from it. The other legacy that FESTAC 77 left behind was the National Theatre complex, Iganmu, Lagos state, built specifically to host the festival and later dedicated to the promotion, preservation and projection of the rich cultural heritage of Nigeria.

As noted earlier, the success of the National Festival of Arts and Culture, particularly the maiden edition in 1970, led to the establishment of structures such as the Council for Arts and Culture at the state levels (see Figure 6.2 darker-coloured states). Arinze (2001) noted that the councils were established to further the objectives of promoting, projecting and propagating the cultural endowment of the states. With the creation of more states between 1987 and 1996 by successive governments, this brought the total number of states in Nigeria to 36 including Abuja,

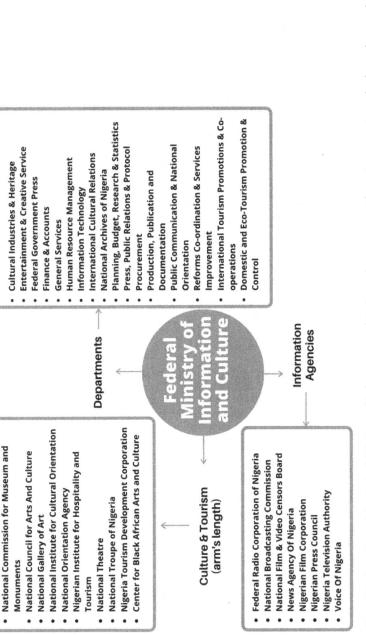

Federal Ministry of Information and Culture

Departments
- Cultural Industries & Heritage
- Entertainment & Creative Service
- Federal Government Press
- Finance & Accounts
- General Services
- Human Resource Management
- Information Technology
- International Cultural Relations
- National Archives of Nigeria
- Planning, Budget, Research & Statistics
- Press, Public Relations & Protocol
- Procurement
- Production, Publication and Documentation
- Public Communication & National Orientation
- Reforms Co-ordination & Services Improvement
- International Tourism Promotions & Co-operations
- Domestic and Eco-Tourism Promotion & Control

Culture & Tourism (arm's length)
- National Commission for Museum and Monuments
- National Council for Arts And Culture
- National Gallery of Art
- National Institute for Cultural Orientation
- National Orientation Agency
- Nigerian Institute for Hospitality and Tourism
- National Theatre
- National Troupe of Nigeria
- Nigeria Tourism Development Corporation
- Center for Black African Arts and Culture

Information Agencies
- Federal Radio Corporation of Nigeria
- National Broadcasting Commission
- National Film & Video Censors Board
- News Agency Of Nigeria
- Nigerian Film Corporation
- Nigerian Press Council
- Nigeria Television Authority
- Voice Of Nigeria

Figure 6.1 Overview of the Federal Ministry of Information and Culture: departments; information agencies and other culture and tourism bodies.

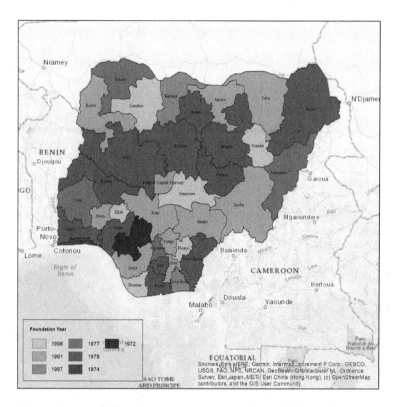

Figure 6.2 Map of Nigeria and its states according to the date in which they established their State Councils for Arts and Culture. Darker, the first phase (1972–1977) and in lighter colours, the second phase (1987–1996). Two states (Edo★ and Adamawa★) are marked according to the date of establishment of their original SCAC, when they were part of larger states (respectively, Bendel and Gongola).

Nigeria's federal capital city and accordingly, additional Councils for Arts and Culture were established (see Figure 6.2, lighter-coloured states).

Generally, the SCAC exists to preserve, promote, project and protect the cultural heritage of states including the promotion of tourism potentials. In terms of function, there are statutory functions that cut across the various councils, which are summarised under the following headings:

a. Cultural Promotions: each State Council is expected to promote the rich cultural heritage of the state through music, dance, theatre and other forms of arts including organising festivals and exhibitions of arts at the local level. One of the ways that councils have achieved this objective is by setting up of state performing arts troupes comprising dancers, musicians and actors who express the cultural heritage of the state mainly through dance, music and drama. The other means of cultural promotion is participation in national and international festivals and honouring performance invitations usually extended by diplomatic missions.

b. Cultural Preservation: each SCAC is expected to manage a facility designated as Arts Theatre or Cultural Centre. The facility is expected to house galleries, studios for artists to create works and a museum.

c. Talent Development: it is the responsibility of each SCAC to discover talent at the grassroots level. One way this is achieved is by organising talent hunt programmes and festivals where these talents are discovered, recruited and trained.

d. Advisory Role: each SCAC has the responsibility for the development of arts and culture at the grassroots level and usually advises the government on matters relating to arts and culture and the implementation of both the state and the national cultural policy.

e. Consultancy Services: each SCAC is expected to offer consultancy services to public and private cultural institutions and in most cases, they act as commissioned regulatory agencies for artists and related interest groups.

f. Revenue Generation: each SCAC is expected to generate revenue through the sale of cultural products such as crafts, textiles and theatrical performances by the state cultural troupe.

Although it appears from the summary above that the State Councils have a general mandate, some engage in distinctive programming, plans and actions that impact on local cultures and development. For instance, the Benue, Rivers, Ogun, Kwara, Nassarawa, Cross Rivers, Oyo, and Ekiti State Councils organise local festivals to promote culture at the grassroots level. They also maintain art and craft centres for skill acquisition, production and sales of crafts, traditional fabrics and cultural products that are peculiar to their state. For instance, Ogun SCAC maintains an expansive local fabric, *Adire* (tie and dye) shop while the Kogi SCAC maintains a traditional carving and weaving shop, which are aimed at contributing to the creative economy of the state. However, of all the SCACs, only a few states including

Niger, Edo, Ogun and in particular Oyo (Adejumo, 2018) have shown through their specific activities and objectives which include a talent hunt (for Artistic Talent) in the State`s rural and urban communities, participation in national exhibitions and international cultural competitions in arts and culture and the generation of revenue for the State (including the multiplier effect on the populace) that they are focused on wealth creation through the creative and cultural industries (CCIs) (www.oyostate.gov.ng). Evidence of their commitment to promote the cultural heritage of the state while also building capacity and generating revenue, is found in the state operating one of the most purpose-built arts and craft centres (Adejumo, 2018). The arts and craft centres serve a dual purpose of the sale of arts and craft and skill acquisition (Adejumo, 2018). Indeed, the Oyo Council for Arts and Culture asserts in its mission statement that it aims to develop the various arts and crafts, artistic talents and good traditional practices of the people to present the state in good light and generate increased development (www.oyostate.gov.ng). Adejumo (2018) observes that the council has translated its mission into action with the establishment of the arts and craft centres and the various talent and community development initiatives in the form of festivals organised in recent times across the local government areas in the state.

Considering the recruitment policies of the majority of the councils, it is safe to say that they impact job creation and economic empowerment at the community level because most of their artists and craftsmen are selected from across local communities based on specific needs of the councils from time to time. Although many councils are not in a good financial state today due to the commercialisation and self-sustaining policy adopted by most state governments, they remain one of the longest-lasting human archival sources of the history for each state because their present and past activities impact and interact with the economic, political, social and cultural lives of the people. Former Director of the Kogi SCAC Jonathan Okpanachi (2020) explained that the commercialisation and self-sustaining policy required the state arts councils to depend on internally generated revenues to run their operations. According to him, the policy meant an end to statutory subventions and allocation by government to the councils, which based on their current economic value provide a veritable incremental source of employment, revenue and growth. Okpanachi observed that the policy has made the councils, which are a major part of the country's creative and cultural industries, 'lame' and unable to contribute more to the creative economy.

The emergence of the NCAC

NCAC was established in 1975 and upgraded in 1987 (Maidugu and Ben-Iheanacho, 2014). It is a Federal Government organisation responsible for the coordination, development and promotion of the rich cultural endowment of the country. It serves as a coordinating agency for cultural activities and a rallying point for all the Arts Councils in Nigeria through national-based activities like the National Arts Festival, better known as NAFEST. All its main activities are summarised in Figure 6.3.

Major annual events of the NCAC and use of culture for development

The African Arts and Crafts Expo (AFAC), launched in 2008, has been a major catalyst in the move towards integrating the arts and culture towards a viable creative economy. As at the 2017 edition, over 15 West African countries participated with 20 states in Nigeria and some NGOs. Through the AFAC, the NCAC has continued to build regional, continental networks for the growth of the Nigerian, African and international creative economy. A recent initiative of the current Chief Executive,

National Council for Arts and Culture (NCAC)

BUSINESS STRUCTURE	PROJECTS	MAJOR EVENTS
The Management of the Council is made up by the Executive Director/ CEO and Seven (7) Directors heading their respective departments as listed below: • Corporate and Strategic Planning • Arts and Crafts • Finance and Accounts • Performing Arts • Research and Documentation • Extension Services • Human Resources Management	**National Research Centres on Specialized Cultural Manifestations:** • National Research Centre on Boat Regatta Traditions • National Research Centre on Durbar Traditions • National Research Centre on Masquerade Traditions • National Research Centre on Textile Traditions **Crafts Development and Skills Acquisition Centres** • Bauchi • Kano • Lagos • Awka • Maiduguri • Sokoto • Ikare	1. The African Arts and Crafts (AFAC) Expo 2. Bi-Annual Meeting of the Chief Executives of Culture of the Federation (CEC) 3. The National Festival of Arts and Culture (NAFEST) 4. The National Culture Quiz Competition for Secondary Schools in Nigeria 5. Indigenous Cuisines Development 6. Local and International Exhibitions 7. The Culture of Peace and Dialogue Forum 8. NCAC Annual Honours Lecture and Award Series

Figure 6.3 Overview of NCAC activities.

Otunba Segun Runsewe, is the expansion and renaming of the AFAC to the International Arts and Crafts Expo (INAC), which expanded globally in 2017. The 2019 expo held between November 20th and 24th broke new ground with 30 countries participating. It also featured components including free skill acquisition, free medical services, waste to wealth initiative and an investment forum.

Indeed, with INAC and its flagship programme, the annual National Festival of Arts and Culture involving all the States of the Federation and the Federal Capital Territory, Abuja, the NCAC has continued to leverage Nigeria's arts and crafts as veritable resources for promoting national unity and integration. In addition, as a catalyst for job and wealth creation, which is reflected in the statement by His Royal Majesty, Omo N'Oba N'Edo Uku Akpolokpolo, Ewuare II, the Oba of Benin while welcoming Otunba Segun Runsewe, the Director-General of the NCAC and his team prelude to the 2019 edition of the annual festival, "the ancient city would have a lifetime opportunity to showcase its culture and further boost its economy" (*The Humanitarian*, 2019: 15). NCAC has been exploiting NAFEST for cultural and national unity purposes while also contributing significantly to the creative economy. Held annually, NAFEST has assumed the status of a primal cultural festival ensuring continuity and progressive updating of traditional skills and sports as a means of enhancing national self-reliance and self-sufficiency. Bello (as cited in Alhamdu, 2008) asserts the festival had its origin in the local festivals of arts staged at various centres before Nigeria's independence in 1960. Bello, however, noted that the festival was limited at the early stages to the visual arts: paintings, craft, sculpture and pottery. He also clarified that it was in 1970 that the first Nigerian Festival of Arts was staged in Lagos and it was expanded to include other aspects of Nigeria's CCIs such as drama, dance, traditional wrestling, weaving and boat regatta (Alhamdu, 2008: 76). Since its launch in 1970, NAFEST has remained the nation's major cultural activity with participation from all the States and the Federal Capital Territory (FCT). Since its inception, the festival has also been organised around a single theme to harness the cultural potentials for national development (Maidugu, Ben-Iheanacho and Iyimoga, 2012).

Over the years, NAFEST has been presented under different themes. The themes from 1970 to 1988 were quite opaque and in many instances only reflected the major performance activities of the festival. For example, 'Dance' was the theme for 1970, 1971, 1972, 1974 and 1988, while 'Visual Arts' was the theme for 1982. The themes from 1989 until 2019 in Edo state have been more dynamic and goal-driven, sometimes as a tie-in to the slogans of the government of the day: 'Culture and National Economic Recovery' (1989), 'Culture and Democracy' (1992) and

Cultural Industries and Economic Empowerment' (2010). The details of the past themes of the festival with the venues and the year they took place are reproduced in Table 6.1.

NAFEST themes and their impacts

A cursory examination of some of the themes of NAFEST indicate that the National Arts Festival from 1970 until 2003 focused on presenting the forum for the propagation of the multifaceted cultures of the Nigerian people as a means of promoting unity in diversity. However, starting from 2004 in Kaduna, the theme 'Using Culture to Build the Nation', signals a new focus on wealth creation through arts and culture, which continues to be a reoccurring philosophy of the festival. For instance, the 2016 NAFEST theme 'Exploring the Goldmine Inherent in Nigeria's Creative Industry' clearly challenged the nation's collective resourcefulness to provide alternative roadmaps out of the current national economic recession. The current Director-General of the NCAC Otunba Segun Runsewe[1] (2019), is of the opinion that the abundant potential of their diverse cultural manifestations if properly harnessed and developed can gainfully engage teeming youths and women who are both rural and urban based. In this way, the sector can contribute meaningfully to attaining the economic diversification agenda of the government. Findings reveal, however, that apart from attempts by participating states to integrate the themes into their presentational materials and the colloquium, the themes often do not drive any long-term agenda and often lose currency at the end of the festival. The participating states return home after the festival and there are no signs, apart from touring with their performing troupe and performing at civic events, that they can consolidate and chart a new course that will expose the potential of the cultural sector and/or the economic value of Nigeria's CCIs. It does seem that some participating states return and look forward to the next edition without applying culture to economic development or exploring the theme as a way to showcase the vital role of culture in national development and economic diversification. Jonathan Okpanachi[1] (2020) shares similar sentiments when he alluded that for some SCACs, the NAFEST has become "something of an annual ritual where the councils unpack after each edition and wait for the next edition with no plans to exploit the themes beyond what is presented during the festival".

In its present state, the NCAC could apply subtle diplomacy to channel the councils towards the encouragement and growth of the creative economy by emphasising healthy competitions and rivalry amongst the states. For instance, in the NAFEST year that positioned CCIs as economic

Table 6.1 Past themes and locations of NAFEST (1970–2019).

Year	Venue	Theme
Cultural development: focus on the development of cultural fields		
1970	Lagos	Dance
1971	Ibadan	Dance
1972	Kaduna	Dance
1974	Kaduna & Lagos	Dance and Music
1982	Port Harcourt	Visual Arts
1983	Maiduguri	Literary Arts
1988	Lagos	Dance
1989	Bauchi	Culture and National Economic Recovery
1990	Kaduna	Promotion of Crafts and National Cultural Development
1992	Abuja	Culture and Democracy
1994	Calabar	African Fashion and Textiles
1995	Abeokuta	The Arts of Metal Technology in Nigeria
Culture as nation-building and promotion		
1996	Jos	Marketing Nigeria's Culture through Crafts
1997	Abuja	Culture and the Art of Communication
1999	Abuja	The Past in the Future: Culture and Development in the New Millennium
2002	Port Harcourt	Celebrating the Culture of Peace and Dialogue
2003	Owerri	Nigeria: Our People, Our Art and Our Heritage
2004	Kaduna	Using Culture to Build the Nation
2005	Abeokuta	Culture as a Tool for National Reform
2006	Yenagoa	Culture, Job Creation and Youth Empowerment
2007	Makurdi	Job Creation and Youth Empowerment
2008	Enugu	Culture and the Challenges of our time: Promoting the Nigerian Dress Culture
Culture and Development as a Creative Economy		
2009	Minna	Culture and the Challenges of Our Time: Cultural Industries and Wealth Creation
2010	Uyo	Cultural Industries and Economic Empowerment
2011	Calabar	Nigerian Traditional Music: A Vehicle for Economic Transformation and Unity
2012	Ilorin	Culture, Peace and Economic Empowerment
2013	Yenagoa	Culture, Peace and National Transformation
2014	Abakaliki	Celebrating Nigeria @ 100: The Role of Culture as a Tool for National Unity
2016	Uyo	Exploring the Goldmine in Nigeria's Creative Industries
Culture as a broader discussion on heritage and national development		
2017	Kaduna	Nigeria: Peace and Unity – Our Pride
2018	Port Harcourt	Our Festivals, Our Heritage
2019	Benin City	Our Royalty, Our Pride

Source: Table retrieved from the Programme of Events 31st National Festival of Arts and Culture (NAFEST), 19th to 26th October, 2019 held in Benin City, Edo State.

goldmines, NCAC as the convener and the coordinating institution of cultural activities and other cultural agencies in the country could have encouraged states to develop creative and innovative steps aimed at fully exploring the theme of each festival. States could have been encouraged to create markets for creative products, which could have then generated a beehive of economic activities through the attendant's local and foreign exchange earnings as well as job creation. In the same vein, states could be encouraged to host art and crafts expos as well as festivals at the grassroots level for economic benefits in their respective states. This would be in addition to establishing more theatres, galleries and other monuments of historical significance to attract tourists with the attendant positive implications including projecting the CCIs as an economic goldmine.

In spite of the expected positive role that the SCACs are expected to play in the development of arts and culture at the grassroots level, the councils are faced with challenges. The most obvious is connected to lack of support for the activities of the council and poor funding due to the self-sustaining policy introduced by most state governments (Adejumo, 2018). For agencies which were hitherto considered least funded, the self-sustaining policy makes it impossible for them to meet their statutory mandate because, by implication, the councils are expected to fund their operations from their internally generated revenue. Edosomwan (2010: 4) explains the self-sustaining policy as it relates to the Edo SCAC:

> government no longer gave subventions to the council for the payment of salaries and allowances of workers and overhead for the prosecution of its programmes. This was a rash decision as it did not take into account, the viability of the council.

Given the policy in place and government declaration that it had no more funds to service other projects outside of its debt burden, councils had no choice but to adjust to their economic expenditure. The reality, as foremost Theatre Scholar and Dramatist Ahmed Yerima observed, is the continued practice of 'tokenism' by past and present governments and supervising ministries and departments, which hinders the growth and progress of most of the councils (Yerima, 2003). Former Benue State Director of Culture Richard Tsevende[1] (2020) explained that tokenism takes the form of monies released for participation at state and national events. In his words:

> apart from the salaries of staff that are paid centrally, we don't receive budgetary allocations for our overheads and for the promotion and

preservation of our rich cultural heritage. It is the little we get from funds we get to prepare for state or national events that we use to stay afloat. This should not be the case. The councils ought to be well funded with funds provided for its operations. Governments at federal and state level have the responsibility of promoting the arts. If that is the case, then they must fund, develop and support the councils to achieve their full potentials.

Indeed, the poor funding situation and the lip service paid to the affairs of culture negatively impacted the growth of the culture industry in Nigeria (Yerima, 2003). There is no doubt that if provided with an enabling environment and support both from the public and private sectors as is the practice in most advanced countries, the various Councils for Arts and Culture, would be capable of creating a new generation of artists and craftsmen who could take advantage of the social media and sell their talents and crafts beyond their local communities for their common good.

Conclusions

This chapter traced the emergence and enumerated the functions of the various Councils for Arts and Culture in Nigeria from the 1970s to the present. It identified the specific roles that some of the SCACs located in the six geo-political zones of Nigeria along with the NCAC have played in community development. The chapter also assessed the various impacts that both the NCAC and the SCACs have had in this area. However, as the chapter observed these councils have had a chequered history of dependency on the whims and caprices of the political leaders, thus making them incapable of genuinely growing into their full potential, reinforcing the evaluation by Edosomwan (2010) of the Edo SCAC. Similarly, although enabling laws that established the numerous Arts Councils in Nigeria look good on paper, the provisions of the enabling law have not been fully exploited largely due to a culture of lip service paid to culture. This is evidenced by the lack of budgetary allocation to the sector and in some cases politicisation of the headship of the agencies in the cultural sector. These have contributed to many challenges these cultural institutions are faced with. To this end, this chapter recommends a drastic change of the funding models by the various states so that councils for arts are adequately funded all year round, enabling them to run and maintain their various activities, which aid in the creation of a creative economy in their respective communities.

Note

1 The research team discussed the issues addressed in the chapter with three policy-makers and key experts: Former Director of Kogi State Council for Arts and Culture Mr. Jonathan Okpanachi (March 18, 2020); Former Director of Culture, Benue State Mr. Richard Tsevende (March 18, 2020); Director General of the National Council For Arts And Culture Otunba Segun Runsewe (December 28, 2019).

References

Adejumo, B. (2018). Role of the council for arts and culture in achieving sustainable development goals: A case study of Oyo State Council for Arts and Culture. Diss. Babcock University.

Aig-Imoukhuede, F. (2006). The Nigerian cultural policy: Analysis, implementation and projections. In *Perspectives in Nigeria's Cultural Diplomacy*. Abuja: National Institute for Cultural Orientation (NICO), Print.

Akogun, T. (2003). Establishment of national directorate of culture. In *Giant Stride*, *1 & 2* (No 24). Lagos: VBO International Limited.

Alhamdu, H. (2008). Evaluation of the contributions of the national council for arts and culture to national development. Retrieved from https//www.kubanni-abu-edu-ng.

Arinze, E. (2001). Culture and national development in Nigeria. In *NCAC Newsletter, Vol 4* (No 1123). Abuja-Nigeria: National Council for Arts and Culture.

Asiwaju (1990, July 30) Imperatives and problems of policy formulation and implementation in the cultural sector. Paper presented at the National Workshop on Nigeria Cultural Parameters in Decision Making organized by NCAC at NIPSS, Kuru, Jos, Plateau State.

Ayakoroma, B. (2015). Effective cultural administration in a globalized economy: Between the person, the organization and the programmes. In Ayakoroma, B (ed.) *Effective Cultural Administration in Nigeria: A Critical Source Book*. Ibadan: Kraft books.

CPN. (1988). *Cultural Policy of Nigeria*. Lagos: Federal Government Press.

Edosomwan, A. (2010). Art and culture administration: The Edo state experience. Retrieved from https://docplayer.net/42375664-Art-and-culture-administration-the -edo- state experience.html.

Edosomwan, A. (2019). Art and culture administration: The Edo state experience. Retrieved from https://docplayer.net/42375664-Art-and-culture-administratio n-the-edo-state experience.html.

Jegede, E. (2015). Cultural imperatives for sustainable development in Nigeria. *International Journal of Humanities and Social Science*, 10(1): 13–24.

Kimanuka, O. (2016). Why culture is vital in a nation's development. Retrieved from https://www.newtimes.co.rw/section/read/202542.

Lagos State Council for Arts and Culture. Retrieved from https://artandculture. lagosstate.gov.ng/.

Maidugu, M., & Ben-Iheanacho, E. (2014). *Arts and Crafts in Nation-Building: Proceedings from the African Arts and Crafts (AFAC) Expo's Investment Forum (2008– 2014)*. Abuja: National Council for Arts and Culture.

Maidugu, M., Ben-Iheanacho, E., & Iyimoga, C. (Eds). (2012). *A Compendium of NAFEST Colloquium 2004–2009*. Ibadan: Kraft Books Limited.

Obafemi, O. (2005, August 14). Role of culture in national development. In *Keynote Speech Presented at the NICO Roundtable on Culture Organised by the National Institute of Cultural Orientation (NICO)*, Abuja.

Okpanachi, J. (2020, March 18) Personal Interview.

Oyo State Council for Arts and Culture. Retrieved from https://oyostate.gov.ng/oyo-state-council-for-arts-and-culture/.

Runsewe, O. (2019, December 28) Personal Interview.

The Humanitarian Magazine. (2019, October). 'Edo NAFEST 2019 Special Edition.' Vol 1 (No 2).

Udoh, B. (2003, August 27). Culture, economy and national development. Paper Presented at the Collaborative National Conference on Refocusing National Policy on Economy Held at the University of Lagos, August 27–29, 2003.

Uyah, A. (2006). World decade for cultural development in Nigeria: Implications for development. In *Perspectives in Nigeria's Cultural Diplomacy*. Abuja: National Institute for Cultural Orientation (NICO).

Williams, R. (1976). *Keywords: A Vocabulary of Culture and Society*. New York: Oxford.

Wilson, N. (2020). *The Space that Separates: A Realist Theory of Art*. Abingdon: Routledge.

Wilson, N., Gross, J., Dent, T., Conor, B., & Comunian, R. (2020). *Re-thinking Inclusive and Sustainable Growth for the Creative Economy: A Literature Review*. DISCE Publications. Retrieved from https://disce.eu/wp-content/uploads/2020/01/DISCE-Report-D5.2.pdf.

Yerima, A. (2003, April 29) Performing art companies and the challenges of the 20th century. In *Keynote Paper Presented at the 2003 Edition of the World Dance Day Organised by the Guild of Nigerian Dancers (GOND)*.

7 The historical evolution of the cultural and creative economy in Mahikeng, South Africa

Implications for contemporary policy

James Drummond and Fiona Drummond

Introduction

The cultural and creative economy is increasingly viewed as a crucial driver of economic growth and employment. A cultural and creative industries (CCIs) development agenda has been adopted across most of the developed world guided by policy documents and development initiatives as well as a wealth of academic, government and industry research (Gregory and Rogerson, 2018: 32). The geographic divide has been changing as the global South has begun researching the CCIs and adopting a creative economy (CE) development agenda. This is true for South Africa, wherein the national government have identified the CCIs as the economy's "new gold" based on their potential to spur economic growth and job opportunities (Mzansi Golden Economy Guidelines, 2016: 5). The CCIs are particularly important to South Africa as a potential growth and development catalyst in an otherwise moribund national economy, as the country struggles with unemployment (29% in 2019), poverty and poor economic growth (0.8% in 2018) (Statistics South Africa, 2020).

However, in order to derive the benefits of economic growth and development, the CCIs need to co-locate in sufficiently high numbers and form clusters. For South Africa, policy and research efforts have largely followed trends set by the global North, focusing on CCIs clusters in large urban centres with relatively high levels of economic development and growth and are able to attract talented creative individuals (Florida, 2002: 743). Accordingly, CCIs clusters have been identified in inner-city Johannesburg (South Africa's largest city) where they have mainly been harnessed for urban renewal. For example, the Maboneng precinct in Johannesburg's inner-city was driven by a single private-property developer who transformed derelict buildings into an arts complex, housing, studios, galleries, office spaces and a museum (Gregory, 2016: 163–165). Additional outdoor creative spaces, entertainment venues, restaurants, hotels and residential accommodation were later developed in the hope that a vibrant, more permanent community would form around the precinct (Gregory, 2016: 163–165).

Not far from the Maboneng precinct is the Newtown Cultural Arc. The Arc encompasses the University of the Witwatersrand, the famous Market Theatre, the Johannesburg Theatre, Museum Africa, commercial art galleries, live music venues, creative office spaces as well as the Constitution Hill precinct which is a mixed-use area including heritage sites, law offices, museums, exhibitions and performance spaces (Pieterse and Gurney, 2012: 197–201). However, the Newtown Cultural Arc has been criticised for lacking an appropriate private-public sector mix and failing to include the local community. Poor planning, and a focus on generating profitable property returns, have also been blamed for stunting organic creativity and cultural resonance (Pieterse and Gurney, 2012: 200–202).

The Maboneng precinct and Newtown Cultural Arc are illustrative of the different types of CCIs activity and cluster management systems that can be found in South Africa. Currently, there is no consensus on the best management strategy for CCIs clusters as each cluster possesses different regional characters and assets as well as challenges (Chapain and Comunian, 2010: 715). Brooks and Kushner (2001: 8) identified five types of management systems for cultural districts in America (designation, development, donation, direction and domination) with differing degrees of state intervention ranging from laissez-faire to centralised directive management. Nevertheless, CCIs clusters are said to require effective leadership and close collaboration between a wide range of actors, including the public, private, community and voluntary sectors, in order to increase their chances of success (ibid.). In general, CCIs clusters will assume "a hybrid form of cultural governance" as the combination of public and private sector intervention allows for more flexibility in response and adaptation to rapidly changing urban economic and policy developments (Mommaas, 2004: 530–531). Mixed-use CCIs clusters are also the most common in South Africa, especially in small towns which include a range of CCIs activities suited to non-metropolitan spaces (Drummond and Snowball, forthcoming).

Research that has begun into non-metropolitan spaces of South Africa is derivate of CE scholarship in the global North. For instance, Gregory and Rogerson (2018: 37–38) studied how several CCIs clusters formed in the Northern suburbs of Johannesburg rather than the inner city. However, it is not just suburbs within large cities that are capable of hosting CCIs clusters. There is a substantial body of cultural tourism literature which suggests that CCIs are important economic and developmental engines in rural areas via their cultural tourism attractions (Richards, 2011: 1239). Hoogendoorn and Visser (2016: 99) described tourism as a major economic driver in South African small towns and a favoured component of post-productivist economic activity and policy discourse. Consequently, Drummond and Snowball (2019: 116) showed how CCIs clusters have formed in rural, small-town spaces of the Eastern Cape province. Their findings echo those of Chapain and Comunian (2010: 115) in suggesting that the potential for rural CCIs clustering is based on the small town's characteristics such as having: larger proportions of the creative class and consumer bases for CCIs goods and services; tourism industries based on local histories, cultures and landscapes; greater socio-economic development levels; more diverse local economies; and better infrastructure (Drummond and Snowball, 2019: 116). In considering the various CCIs activities potentially found in clusters, it is reasonable to suggest that they will each require different types of management systems with varying combinations of government, private sector and community involvement. Thus, in order to evaluate which mixes of CCIs activity and cultural governance have worked best, it is useful to take a historical approach.

This chapter extends the insights into rural small-town CCIs clustering developed by Drummond and Snowball (2019) by examining the ebb and flow of CCIs cluster development in Mahikeng, the capital city of the North-West province, during the era of the former Bophuthatswana Bantustan from 1977 to 1994. The subsequent demise of Mahikeng's cluster post 1994 illustrates both the importance of continuous government support and how a cluster's initial development influences its long-term sustainability. This research takes a historical perspective towards understanding the development of the CE through an African context, which hitherto has been relatively neglected.

Context and methods

Mahikeng, meaning "place of stones" in the local Setswana language, is a medium-sized town and is currently the capital of the North-West Province (see Figure 7.1). The town has a complex history as it was a place of intersection between the local African Batswana people, the British under colonial rule and the Afrikaners (before and during apartheid). The first settlement on the site was founded by the Tshidi Rolong people under the name Mahikeng in 1881. Since it was on the imperial

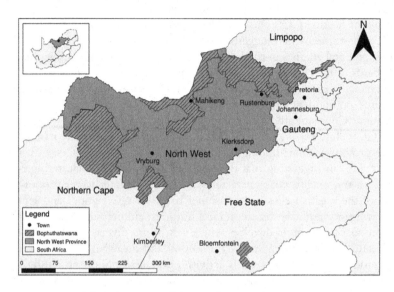

Figure 7.1 Mahikeng location and the North-West province.

road between Cape Town and Rhodesia, the British sought to secure the area and formed a colonial town adjacent to the African settlement in 1886 which they named Mafeking and which served as the capital of the Bechuanaland Protectorate from 1896 to 1966 (Nel and Drummond, 2019: 88). This was the first capital status that the town would be bestowed. When the Bechuanaland Protectorate gained independence from Britain in 1966, the capital was moved to Gaborone in the newly independent Botswana. Mafeking then became part of the Union of South Africa which had been under Afrikaner governance since 1910 (Drummond and Parnell, 1991: 164). Until this point, Mafeking had managed to remain apart from strict apartheid enforcement of racial segregation due to the presence of Britain as a colonial power, but, with the withdrawal of the British, Mafeking felt the full force of apartheid legislation (Drummond and Parnell, 1991: 164).

During the 1960s and 1970s, South Africa entered a phase of 'grand apartheid' which involved stringently enforcing racial segregation through social engineering. Black Africans were forcibly removed from 'White' South Africa to their 'traditional' rural 'homelands' or 'bantustans'. Four 'bantustans' (Bophuthatswana, Ciskei, Transkei and Venda) were granted independence from South Africa and given budgetary support from the apartheid government in order to support their sham 'independence' as they were not recognised as being legal or separate from South Africa by the international community. The most successful of the four 'bantustans' was Bophuthatswana, the so-called 'traditional homeland' of the Batswana people. Bophuthatswana was established in 1977 with Mmabatho as its capital under 'president' Lucas Mangope.

Mmabatho was only seven kilometres from Mafeking and uniquely, for 'White' South African towns, the local White population of Mafeking voted to be incorporated into the Black African-ruled Bophuthatswana 'bantustan' in 1980 as they wanted to regain the prosperity associated with being a capital because Mmabatho and Mafeking effectively functioned as one town (Drummond and Parnell, 1991: 167). When Mafeking was incorporated into Bophuthatswana, the town name was changed to Mafikeng to move away from the anglicised spelling and better represent the Setswana language.

The combined town of Mafikeng-Mmabatho became a 'bantustan boomtown' as the capital of Bophuthatswana (Drummond and Parnell, 1991: 167). Bophuthatswana's economy was based on agriculture, platinum mining, casino tourism and construction, as major infrastructure projects associated with the trappings of a capital city in a newly 'independent' African country were undertaken including an airport, a sports stadium and complex, a university, government buildings, two hotels, radio and TV stations and a cultural centre (Dixon Soule Associates, 1987; Drummond and Parnell, 1991: 168–169; Nel and Drummond, 2019: 88–89). The arts and culture sector was prioritised by Mangope who regarded it as being "crucial", stating that "the success of a society is not measured only by the level of nutrition and employment, but also by the level of creativity" (Dixon Soule Associates, 1987: 150). In effect, the investment in cultural infrastructure projects created a CCIs cluster in the combined town of Mafikeng-Mmabatho.

Mafikeng's fortunes were to change again in 1994 when South Africa gained democracy and the 'bantustans' were disbanded. This caused considerable unease in the town as Mafikeng's capital status hung in the balance, and it faced competition from surrounding larger towns to be the North-West province's new capital. The new African National Congress (ANC) government confirmed that Mafikeng (including Mmabatho) would retain its capital status for the North-West province following the 1994 election. However, this would not be enough to save the town from recession as the new government set about dismantling the legacy of apartheid, including that which had been built in the 'bantustans'. Consequently, while much of South Africa flourished in the post-apartheid environment, Mafikeng suffered as cultural institutions languished without state funding and support.

A decade later, following the 2004 elections, the ANC government committed to supporting economic growth and development in the town. ANC efforts resulted in another boom for Mafikeng and local entrepreneurs attempted to revive cultural and creative activity. However, the boom was short-lived as the Global 2008/2009 Financial Crisis sent the town into a slump from which it has yet to completely recover. Furthermore, as part of the dismantling of apartheid and reclaiming African heritage, the name of the town returned to that of the original African settlement of Mahikeng in 2012. During this time there was a renewed state-led effort to promote culture-led development through celebrating the Batswana culture as embodied by the Mahika-Mahikeng Festival (Drummond et al., 2020 in press). Despite these efforts, government incapacity, corruption and economic development failures (including an attempt at culture-led development) have contributed to the sustained slump in Mahikeng and resulted in anti-government protests in 2018 which turned violent (Shange, 2018). Mahikeng's CCIs cluster has felt the effects of these political and economic phases of the town's history and has gone from prosperity to near collapse, with an attempt at revival along the way.

This chapter, therefore, delves back into Mahikeng's history by using a combination of three research methods. The first is an auto-ethnographic account from James Drummond who has lived in and researched Mahikeng since 1984. He has thus become an "accidental research participant" as he has seen, experienced and researched Mahikeng over time (Shaw, 2013: 1). In recounting his personal oral histories relating to the town's CE, the researcher's intentions are to use his auto-biographical accounts as a means of documenting and understanding contemporary transformations of Mahikeng's CCIs cluster in accordance with the practice of cultural geography (Söderström, 2010: 115). The insights gained from this auto-ethnographic process were further verified and triangulated through archival research from mid-2019 onwards into local and national press articles, news reports and government publications as well as two field audits of the CCIs in operation in Mahikeng conducted in 2016 and 2018. The first field audit was conducted in 2016 during the Mahika-Mahikeng Festival which was an attempted revival of the town's CE (Drummond et al., 2020 in press). The second field audit was conducted in 2018 after rioting related to political unrest during which cultural institutions were targeted and damaged (Sefularo, 2018). The archival research and field audits allowed the researchers to track the CCIs cluster through time and determine how it had changed since South Africa's democracy.

Mafikeng in Bophuthatswana (1977–1994): the creation of a CCIs cluster

During the Bophuthatswana era (1977 – 1994), Lucas Mangope's government pushed hard for international recognition of Bophuthatswana as an independent country (rather than as an instrument of apartheid). Linked to this drive for legitimacy was an attempt to turn Mafikeng into a capital city with all the associated infrastructural, institutional and organisational trimmings and trappings expected of an African capital. The CCIs were seen as a crucial part of a capital city and were thus heavily invested in by the Bophuthatswana government, with the development of new cultural institutions taking centre stage. However, this investment was not a deliberate attempt to form a CCIs cluster, which is now a common policy objective amongst global governments. Rather, it was an attempt to legitimise a mock independent country by building the infrastructure and institutions that any global capital city would possess to embolden the claim that Bophuthatswana was separate from South Africa (Lissoni, 2011: 91).

State-of-the-art facilities were a must for Mangope's government. A national broadcaster was established with Radio Bop (1978) broadcasting in English, Radio Mmabatho (1986) broadcasting in Setswana and BopTV (1984) having an expressed mission to educate, inform and entertain (Dixon Soule Associates, 1987: 130). Both the radio and TV stations did their own in-house productions and recruited staff from Johannesburg, Cape Town and the United Kingdom, employing over 250 people by 1987 (Dixon Soule Associates, 1987: 132). While both stations had the ability to transmit across Southern Africa, Radio Bop had almost one million listeners and made a net profit of almost two million Rand by 1985 (Dixon Soule Associates, 1987: 130). Approximately 20% of BopTV's programming was filmed and produced in Bophuthatswana with programmes in both English and Setswana (Dixon Soule Associates, 1987: 131). At a time when it was difficult for Black people to make much headway in South African broadcasting, Radio Bop, Radio Mmabatho and BopTV played an important role in training many of the first generation of Black African presenters and technicians in the post-apartheid South African Broadcasting Corporation (SABC).

Further pushing Mangope's state-of-the-art capital vision, Bophuthatswana Recording Studios was built in 1991 and would later be called the "most lavish recording facility ever built" with three studios, the largest of which could accommodate a full orchestra, and multiple editing suits surrounded by a secure self-contained luxury resort (Robjohns, 2013). The idea behind the recording studios was to raise

Bophuthatswana's profile as a global music industry leader by attracting international music acts to record in a peaceful environment in facilities which rivalled the best studios in the world at that time (Robjohns, 2013). During apartheid, however, the studios struggled as many international artists boycotted them as they did not want to support the institution of apartheid that Bophuthatswana was.

Top-down CCIs clustering in Bophuthatswana was further enhanced by the establishment of the Mmabana Foundation (meaning 'mother of the children' in Setswana) in 1986. As the Bophuthatswana regime had established close ties with Israel as part of its strategy to elicit international recognition as an independent state (Lissoni, 2011: 90), the Israelis were influential in helping to model Mmabana after similar institutions in Israel (Lissoni, 2011: 90; Manson and Mbenga, 2017: 139). The centre housed facilities for both learning and experiencing the arts including dance, music, gymnastics, drama (including hosting national touring performances) and arts & crafts. (Dixon Soule Associates, 1987; Lissoni, 2011; Mmabana Arts, Culture and Sports Foundation, 2011).

Mmabana was headquartered in Mafikeng-Mmabatho but had other smaller satellite centres offering condensed programmes. Instruction in musical instruments was encouraged at Mmabana centres and orchestra members would often travel to rural schools with their instruments to give classes to local children. In terms of dancing, Mmabana in conjunction with the Bophuthatswana Arts Council created a flourishing ballroom and Latin American dance programme. According to Lillian Dooley, director of Bophuthatswana ballroom dancing, "in the twelve different regions of Bophuthatswana, there [were] about five or six clubs in each region" which was all co-ordinated from Mmabatho (Old Dancing Videos, 2020: 16:39). Mmabana produced a number of prominent alumni including a South African tumbling champion (1990–2002), Tseko Mogotsi, rapper Cassper Nyovest, actor Mahlubi Kraai and dance champion and prominent choreographer Tebogo Kgobokoe (Mmabana Arts, Culture and Sports Foundation, 2011; SABC News, 2018).

A number of other CCIs completed the cluster including the University of Bophuthatswana Fine Arts Department which hosted an annual Sol Plaatje Memorial Art Exhibition which showcased work from fine artists from around Bophuthatswana. The university also played a key role in preserving the Setswana language as the Department of Setswana created a dictionary including words, traditional phrases and proverbs that were used by modern Setswana speakers and also those which were no longer in popular usage and were in danger of being lost (Dixon Soule Associates, 1987: 141). The Mafikeng Museum showcased the town's most significant historical events like the siege of Mafeking during the

Anglo-Boer War and the founding of the Boy Scouts by Colonel Robert Baden-Powell. Craft training in dressmaking, silk screening, carpentry, ceramics and jewellery design was also offered through Bophuthatswana's national handicraft project which aimed to train students who would return to the rural areas able to earn an income by satisfying local and tourist markets as well as to teach the skills they had acquired (Dixon Soule Associates, 1987: 150, 153).

The Bophuthatswana government's investment in the CCIs was at a time before the concept of the CE became a global buzzword. Thus, there was no discourse surrounding the CCIs as potential drivers of growth and urban renewal. Consequently, Mafikeng-Mmabatho can be interpreted as a cluster before the terminology to call it such existed. No evidence was uncovered which would have suggested that the Bophuthatswana government, the South African government, or the private sector, made explicit policy decisions to promote a CCIs cluster in Mafikeng-Mmabatho. However, while the conceptual framework and language of the CE had not been developed at the time, Mangope was broadly arguing for investment in the cultural and creative economy centred in the capital. However, this does not negate criticisms of the regime nor the man, as portrayed by Lawrence and Manson (1994: 460–461). Since it was before the CCIs gained recognition as a potential growth driver, the cluster did not benefit from any of the centralised planning or support that has become standard policy and practice nowadays. Despite this, spaces were opened up in Bophuthatswana particularly for Black Africans to develop in the cultural and creative sector and this has been acknowledged by the alumni of Mmabana (SABC News, 2018).

Mahikeng did not benefit from continued government support, planning or funding when the transition was made to the new democratic South Africa, as the cluster was not recognised as a catalyst for growth and development. The mixed nature of CCIs cluster activity in Mahikeng falls in line with other South African CCIs clustering case studies like the Maboneng precinct (Gregory, 2016), Newtown Cultural Arc (Pieterse and Gurney, 2012) and several small towns in the Eastern Cape province (Drummond and Snowball, forthcoming). However, unlike these CCIs clusters, Mahikeng's cluster mainly constituted cultural institutions with relatively few small businesses and was completely state led; the cultural institutions were supported, directed and funded by the Bophuthatswana government from conception, though there was no concerted policy or management effort in terms of CCIs policy. Mahikeng's CCIs cluster therefore falls under Brooks and Kushner's (2001: 7) domination category of cluster management system which is defined as "the administration supports and directs all aspects of [cluster] development and activity". The state domination of the CCIs cluster meant that it was dependent on continued state support for its survival.

Mafikeng in the 'new' South Africa (1994–2018): the demise of the cluster

The 1994 transition to democracy and the re-incorporation of Bophuthatswana into South Africa brought about major disinvestment and initiated the collapse of state-led (Bophuthatswana) promotion of the CE. Bophuthatswana's flourishing cultural institutions were left to flounder without support from the new ANC government, who were seeking to dismantle all associations with apartheid. Each of the aforementioned institutions suffered from a lack of funding, having lost their designation as crucial to the South African government's vision, although they had a number of different experiences when it came to re-incorporation into South Africa.

The Bophuthatswana Broadcasting Corporation comprising Radio Bop, Radio Mmabatho and BopTV were engulfed by the SABC and later downgraded to SABC's North-West province branch, as studios in Johannesburg and Cape Town took over the bulk of the work. The Bophuthatswana Recording Studios were re-branded as Rhino, and leased to the SABC which used it as an in-house recording facility (Robjohns, 2013). With the apartheid connotations no longer hanging over the studio, international customers made use of the facility. Though it had successes – the biggest client was Walt Disney Company who hired the studios to record their award-winning soundtrack for *The Lion King* (1994) – this was short-lived. The SABC did not renew their contract in 2003, leaving Rhino to fall into disuse (Robjohns, 2013). At the time of the field audits in 2016 and 2018, the recording studios, TV and radio stations were all in a state of disuse and neglect and, with no investment for a sustained period of time, have become outdated. Budget cuts and retrenchments have forced many of those who worked at the stations and studios to move elsewhere to find employment.

Manson and Mbenga (2017: 139) pointed out that "four of the five popular and effective Mmabana Cultural Centres established by Mangope [...] quickly re-orientated themselves to broader national objectives" by seeking affiliation with South African arts organisations. Mmabana in Mafikeng suffered from a lack of funds and criticisms from provincial ANC politicians for being Eurocentric and elitist. For instance, their ballet programme entered a gradual decline and stopped being taught completely in 2006 due to a lack of support from Mmabana management and budget cuts. The Bophuthatswana National Orchestra attempted to rebrand itself as the South African Chamber Orchestra, however, it too suffered a Eurocentric critique and failed to survive. Mmabana's drama programme also experienced disinvestment and a lack of support as touring productions ceased to include Mafikeng on their schedule and the staging of local productions became less frequent. The exclusion of Mafikeng from touring productions is illustrative of its cultural downgrade as it has effectively fallen off the radar. Similarly to those who had been employed by the broadcasting corporation and recording studios, Mmabana's performers and teachers also left the town, further contributing to the exodus of creative talent.

With financial cuts at the university (renamed the North-West University), the Department of Fine Arts was closed down in 1996 and the Annual Sol Plaatje Memorial Arts Exhibition abandoned. The once-thriving Department of Setswana now comprises only two members of staff with student numbers drastically shrinking following the introduction of democracy in 1994 (Manson and Mbenga, 2017: 139). The 2016 audit revealed the Mafikeng Museum to be a shell of its former self as most references to the town's colonial past have been packed away into permanent storage or have been damaged. Notably, this included the eternal flame of the Boy Scouts which had been located on the museum grounds and could once again serve as a global heritage opportunity. At present, the South African government feels that it no longer needs a curator to be employed by the museum and the exhibits are in need of updating to reflect the town's African and colonial heritage.

The budget cuts and retrenchments forced talented and skilled Black Africans to leave Mafikeng and move to the big cities that had denied them opportunities during apartheid. Mafikeng's loss of creative talent occurred across the board, thereby drastically weakening the town's CE. At present, the town still has not been able to re-attract talented individuals in large enough numbers to rejuvenate the CE and promote culture-led economic growth and development.

Mahikeng (2018–present): attempted revivals, anti-government protests and the burning of Mmabana

As state-led initiatives collapsed, local African entrepreneurs attempted to fill the cultural and creative void by promoting music festivals and events. Exemplars of this came from the 60s Party and the Legends of House outdoor music festivals which attracted national and international performers as well as crowds from the local area and Johannesburg (Drummond et al., 2020 in press). However, the 60s festival stopped operating partly due to a campaign led by the local newspaper, the *Mahikeng Mail*, critiquing the disorderly and dangerous behaviour associated with the festival attendees. To date, this has been the only private-sector attempt at reviving cultural and creative activity in Mahikeng which was successful for a time. To this end, the origins of Mahikeng's CCIs cluster development through state-led creation, support and funding has effectively harmed the cluster. With no residual state support and no private or community sector willing to step up to the plate, Mahikeng CCIs development has all but stagnated. However, there may be a glimmer of hope as local artists who have become nationally successful are attempting to give back to their home town. For example, during the 2016 audit, a poster advertising a concert at the Mmabatho Stadium, featuring local artists, was organised by one of South Africa's most successful rap and hip-hop artists to date and Mmabana alumni, Cassper Nyovest. It is yet to be seen whether these grassroots attempts at reviving Mahikeng's CE will take off as a successful, albeit initial, injection of interest in the town, whereas attempted state-led revivals like the Mahika-Mahikeng Festival have largely failed.

The Mahika-Mahikeng Festival is a government-driven event that enthusiastically promotes the local Setswana language and Batswana culture by featuring distinct African music, theatre, dance, crafts and exhibition. The 2016 festival was analysed by Drummond et al. (2020 in press), who determined that there was a poor return on investment mainly due to the failure to attract much of an audience from outside of the town or to develop strong local economic linkages with promoters, suppliers, artists or the community. The festival generated significant opposition from local artists, who claimed to have been excluded (Drummond et al., 2020 in press). The 2019 festival was cancelled due to a failure of leadership and corruption charges laid against senior management (Mashigo, 2019). At the time of writing, it seems improbable that the 2020 festival will happen due to the ongoing disruption caused by the COVID-19 pandemic coupled with these systemic issues.

The Mahika-Mahikeng Festival seemed to indicate a renewed commitment by government to support the CCIs and an attempt to harness a cultural event in the pursuit of culture-led development. Given the town's reliance on the state for the CCIs to function let alone flourish, this was a promising outlook for Mahikeng's CE. However, unrest had been growing in the North-West province, and Mahikeng specifically, relating to perceived provincial government corruption and the failure to meet service delivery requirements or promote economic growth (Shange, 2018). Tensions came to a head in April 2018 when anti-government protests turned violent. The Mmabana Foundation in Mahikeng was targeted by protestors and was burnt down, incurring an estimated 50 million Rands worth of damage (SABC News, 2018; Sefularo, 2018).

Figure 7.2 Damages to Mmabana following the 2018 protests (photos: JH Drummond, 2018).

Following the protests, the 2018 audit found that Mmabana was closed to the public and artists alike, with employees having no office space in which to work. To date, no repairs have been done to the building or its contents and it is currently lying derelict (see Figure 7.2). This has further devastated Mahikeng's CE as artists and students are left without a space in which to work and learn.

Concluding remarks and policy recommendations

The historical experience of the CE in Mahikeng offers some disconcerting outcomes. Although unplanned, a non-metropolitan cluster developed in the Bophuthatswana era, thus confirming the findings of Drummond and Snowball (2019: 116) that clusters can emerge in non-metropolitan South Africa. However, Mahikeng's cluster was state-led and did not prosper when the state was transformed and support and funding withdrawn, leading to decline and retrenchments.

Having lost impetus, it has proved difficult to redevelop the cluster from the bottom up and government initiatives to promote the cluster, including through the Mahika-Mahikeng Festival. This suggests that non-metropolitan clusters require some degree of state support and private sector and community buy-in, as no one sector has been able to successfully take up the mantle and maintain the CCIs cluster without the support of the other. Moreover, due to the vulnerability of Mahikeng's cluster to changing political interests, it is important for sustainability that a hybrid form of cluster management including the state, private sector and local community be implemented as suggested by Mommaas (2004: 530–531). If the private sector and community had been involved in cluster governance in Mahikeng during the Bophuthatswana era, the cluster may have evolved differently and innovated in response to the scaling back of state participation after re-incorporation into South Africa. The type of management system implemented should also be informed by the type of CCIs activity within the cluster. For a CCIs cluster like Mahikeng's that is mainly comprised of cultural institutions, continued support and funding by the state is crucial. This is especially true when there are social objectives associated with the cultural institutions as the private sector has the potential to be exclusive.

Currently, these findings do not bode well for the broader CE in South Africa. Mahikeng was not able to sustain a CCIs cluster due to the loss of funding and talented individuals. Similarly, the COVID-19 pandemic has brought about a significant shock to the national arts sector. It will not be easy to recover momentum, and government and the private sector will have to mobilise funding to aid recovery. This will be challenging as governments will need to carefully allocate budgets in the aftermath of COVID-19 and the arts have a history of not being prioritised and underfunded. Failure to adequately support the CCIs would raise the spectre of repeating the failure of the Mahikeng CCIs cluster.

References

Brooks AC and Kushner RJ (2001) Cultural districts and urban development. *International Journal of Arts Management* 3(2): 4–15.

Chapain CA and Comunian R (2010) Enabling and inhibiting the creative economy: The role of the local and regional dimensions in England. *Regional Studies* 43(6): 717–734.

Dixon Soule Associates (1987) *A Nation on the March*. Bophuthatswana: Hans Strydom Publishers.

Drummond F and Snowball J (2019) Cultural clusters as a local economic development strategy in rural small-town areas: Sarah Baartman district in South Africa. *Bulletin of Geography: Socio-Economic Series* 43: 107–119.

Drummond FJ and Snowball J (forthcoming) Rural cultural and creative industry clustering: The Sarah Baartman district, South Africa. In: Hracs BJ, Comunian R and England L (eds) *Spaces and Working Practices for Creative Economies in Africa*. London: Routledge.

Drummond JH and Parnell SM (1991) Mafikeng-Mmabatho. In: Lemon A (ed) *Homes Apart: South Africa's Segregated Cities*. London: Paul Chapman, pp. 162–173.

Drummond JH, Snowball J, Antrobus G and Drummond FJ (2020 in press) The role of cultural festivals in regional economic development: A case study of Mahika Mahikeng. In: Scherf K and Richards G (eds) *Creative Tourism in Smaller Communities*. Calgary: University of Calgary Press.

Florida R (2002) The economic geography of talent. *Annals of the Association of American Geographers* 94(2): 743–755.

Gregory JJ (2016) Creative industries and urban regeneration – The Maboneng precinct, Johannesburg. *Local Economy* 31(1–2): 158–171.

Gregory JJ and Rogerson CM (2018) Suburban creativity: The geography of creative industries in Johannesburg. *Bulletin of Geography: Socio-Economic Series* 39: 31–52.

Hoogendoorn G and Visser G (2016) South Africa's small towns: A review on recent research. *Local Economy* 31(1–2): 95–108.

Lawrence M and Manson AH (1994) The 'dog of the boers': The rise and fall of Mangope in Bophuthatswana. *Journal of Southern African Studies* 20(3): 447–461.

Lissoni A (2011) Africa's 'Little Israel': Bophuthatswana's not-so-secret ties with Israel. *South African Review of Sociology* 42(3): 79–93.

Manson A and Mbenga B (2017) Bophuthatswana and the North West province: From pan-Twsanaism to mineral-based ethnic assertiveness. In: Ally S and Lissoni A (eds) *New Histories of South Africa's Apartheid-Era Bantustans*. Oxford: Routledge, pp. 135–211.

Mashigo L (2019) Mahika Mahikeng tender row threatens to destabilise the North West Province. *The Star*, 6 November 2019. Available at: https://www.iol.co.z a/the-star/news/mahika-mahikeng-tender-row-threatens-to-destabilise-north-w est-province-36746078 (accessed 17 May 2020).

Mmabana Arts, Culture and Sports Foundation (2011) *Mmabana Arts, Culture and Sports Foundation 2011*. Available at: https://www.yumpu.com/en/document/r ead/6376226/details-mmabana (accessed 17 May 2020).

Mommaas H (2004) Cultural clusters and the post-industrial city: Towards the remapping of urban cultural policy. *Urban Studies* 41(3): 507–532.

Mzansi's Golden Economy Guidelines (2016) *Mzansi's Golden Economy (MGE) Guidelines: Criteria, Eligibility, Processes and Systems 2016/2017*. Report, Department of Arts and Culture. Available at: http://www.dac.gov.za/sites/de fault/files/eForms/2016-17-guidelines-for-mzansi-golden-economy-1-0-final.p df (accessed 25 January 2018).

Nel V and Drummond J (2019) Mahikeng: A remote provincial capital with a turbulent history. In: Marais L and Nel V (eds) *Space and Planning in Secondary Cities: Reflections from South Africa*. Bloemfontein: Sun Media, pp. 87–114.

Old Dance Videos (2020) *1990 First Bophuthatswana Open Ballroom and Latin Champs Sun City*. Available at: https://www.youtube.com/watch?v=tfrQqb4y1m4 (accessed 17 May 2020).

Pieterse E and Gurney K (2012) Johannesburg: Investing in cultural economies or publics? In: Anheier H and Isar YR (eds) *Cultures and Globalisation: Cities, Cultural Policy and Governance*. London: SAGE Publications, pp. 194–203.

Richards G (2011) Creativity and tourism: The state of the art. *Annals of Tourism Research* 38(4): 1225–1253.

Robjohns H (2013) The BOP studios story. *Sound on Sound*, October 2013. Available at: https://www.soundonsound.com/music-business/bop-studios-story (accessed 17 May 2020).

SABC News (2018) Mmabana Arts Foundation will need millions to repair. *SABC News*, 3 December 2018. Available at: https://www.sabcnews.com/sabcnews/m mabana-arts-foundation-will-need-millions-to-repair/ (accessed 17 May 2020).

Sefularo M (2018) #Mahikeng: Officials in shock after arts centre torched. *Eyewitness News*. Available at: https://ewn.co.za/2018/04/20/mahikeng-officials-in-shock-after-arts-centre-torched (accessed 16 May 2020).

Shange N (2018) Mayhem in Mahikeng: Looting and loathing in the North West. *Sunday Times*, 19 April 2018. Available at: https://www.timeslive.co.za/news/south-africa/2018-04-19-mayhem-in-mahikeng-looting-and-loathing-in-the-n orth-west/ (accessed 17 May 2020).

Shaw WS (2013) Auto-ethnography and autobiography in geographical research. *Geoforum* 46: 1–4.

Söderström O (2010) Redefining the field: Auto-ethnographic notes. *Cultural Geographies* 18(1): 115–118.

Statistics South Africa (2020) *Statistics South Africa*. Available at: http://www.statssa. gov.za/ (accessed 17 May 2020).

8 Finance for creative and cultural industries in Africa

Yemisi Mokuolu, Victoria Kay and
Claudia María Velilla-Zuloaga

Introduction

Over the past decade, the financing of creative and cultural industries in Africa has acquired new centrality. The CCIs have grown and evolved across their entire supply chain. The balance of trade shows an evolution from Africa as a receiving market of cultural and creative goods to an active producer and contributor: "African cultural content is also increasingly being exported internationally" (UNESCO, 2015: 72). Financing mechanisms and frameworks, as well as the support provided to and required by CCIs businesses, need to evolve accordingly in order to unlock the full potential of the sector.

Africa's economic drivers (namely economic growth, young and rapidly growing demographics, and innovation in digital technology) make it a vibrant investment destination. According to the United Nations Conference on Trade and Development – UNCTAD (2018), the CCIs are amongst the most dynamic sectors in the world economy. When combined with Africa's abundance of talent, rich cultural traditions and heritages, CCIs can offer innovative revenue-generating opportunities to support the economic growth of countries, job-creation and new occupational skills. This, they argue, could result in greater wealth for communities and better social environments. There is, therefore, an urgent need to address the funding and support gaps faced by CCIs, "ensuring that creative industries continue to grow and expand in a way of increasing opportunities and diversity, leading to inclusive growth while adapting to new economic shifts" (UNCTAD, 2018: 32). However, for the opportunity facing CCIs in Africa to be fully realised, allocation of and access to funds and dedicated support must be addressed too. This needs to be connected with a better understanding of the finance ecosystem in which CCIs operate. The remaining challenges, support and financing systems, which are playing catch-up, hamper the true potential of this sector.

Our research shows that successful investments happen when creatives have a full understanding of the mode of investment suited to their business model. This includes brands which have come from reputable existing businesses, have demonstrated positive cashflow and won several pitching rounds but failed to convert investor interest into a willingness to invest. Others redesigned their business models to meet the needs of investors, thus exhausting resources and altering the purpose of their businesses. Although some industries have precise requirements, businesses within the creative economy still need to adhere to their commercial and growth potential. When adopting models that have been developed specifically for their type of business and sector, they have been able to raise investment and provide returns. However, some sectors within the CCIs, including high-growth potential sectors, do not have 'typical' or 'traditional' investment models that are universally understood by investors.

Our current experience[1] has been of a stilted investment flow in CCIs in Africa, attributable not to the lack of capital or investor interest per se, but to a lack of understanding by creatives and investors of investment processes and how these work within CCIs.

This chapter aims to contribute to a better understanding of CCIs as an ecosystem in Africa and the design and implementation of frameworks, tools, policies and partnerships to address current funding needs and gaps sustainably. It by no means intends to cover all aspects of finance for CCIs in Africa. Moreover, this is not a chapter on investment finance. It does, however, present a reflection on the current opportunities and challenges of finance for CCIs in Africa from the perspective of businesses, mentors, investors and third-party providers across several countries and sectors. The themes and concerns expressed resonate across borders and, in most instances, sectors. This reflection, we hope, will provide insights for innovative and collaborative actions, as well as further research and discussion.

Understanding creative and cultural industries, finance and business support

Before turning to the data, it is essential to clarify our working definitions concerning three critical terms used in this chapter and within our research project. Our definition of creative and cultural industries includes the industries listed by the United Kingdom Department of Culture, Media and Sport in their definition of the creative industries (DCMS, 1998). In addition, we also acknowledge the work of the United

Nations Educational, Scientific and Cultural Organisation (UNESCO). Creative and cultural industries are here defined as – industries (from small to large) characterised by the use of creativity and intellectual capital as inputs in the development of goods and services. In our research project, using this definition, we consider the work of writers, music and film companies as well as architecture, fashion and more. The range of businesses and activities included connects to the complexity and challenges of researching this field. While this chapter looks at CCIs overall, we recognise that different industries within the CCIs may follow different financial models and present specific requirements. This will be acknowledged when possible.

We use the term CCIs financing to describe the different ways in which creatives (sole traders and self-employed) and CCIs businesses fund their activities. These, we argue, can be further separated into three main aspects: (1) allocation or disbursement (the financing going to the CCIs); (2) access – the financing ecosystem from the point of view of the businesses and (3) business support – usually key in connecting (1) and (2). Therefore, in this chapter, we will look not only to the finance ecosystem for CCIs but how it interconnects with CCIs business support. This term includes different enabling factors (internal and external to the projects and businesses themselves) required to becoming self-sustainable and to unlock appropriate financing from inception to establishment (Munro, 2017). In our research, we are specifically interested in what support is provided, the experiences of research participants concerning support they have received and then what was missing. We specifically reflect on these current gaps as perceived by the businesses and identify where changes need to be made to enable efficient and impactful financing and business support to CCIs.

Getting a clear picture of the landscape of financing options can be an overwhelming task. Furthermore, the literature highlights how CCIs financing is currently evolving as traditional financing institutions do not offer enough tailor-made solutions for CCIs (Monclus, 2015). However, no such articulations are readily available for CCIs in Africa. There are some key considerations that contribute to our decision to look at funding. Figure 8.2 seeks to provide a simplified general overview of some of the most common financing options according to capital requirements and project/business stage.

Therefore, in this complex context, we firstly want to investigate what finance ecosystem exists for CCIs in Africa and how CCIs interact with it, and secondly how this overlaps or connects with business support that is being provided or might be missing in the sector.

Research methodology and sample

To answer the stated research questions, we gathered the perspectives of 14 stakeholders in our network,[2] including investors, during the course of 2019 through interviews. These were informal and unstructured and as such, aligned with an ethnographic approach to data gathering (Stage and Mattson, 2003). The details of the sample are included in Table 8.1. We seek to present insights from a range of CCIs and countries in Africa and connected to Africa in relation to finance, as well as a balanced sample with consideration to gender. All the discussants had experience with running a business and some also had broader experiences in finance and business development.

Table 8.1 Research sample overview.

#	Sector	City/Country	Gender	Funder/Funded Organisation
1	Writer	Kenya/Canada	M	Funded
2	Music & finance	Kenya	M	Funded
3	Film, music/arts collective, production	Kenya	M	Funded
4	Stand-up/Improv, production, talent management	Kenya	M	Funded
5	Events, media/film & content production	Kenya / USA	Team – M&F	Funded
6	Mentor & investor	Switzerland & Various African Countries	M	Funder
7	Musical theatre	Ghana	F	Funded
8	Architecture, design & innovation	Ghana	F	Funder & funded
9	Policy	Switzerland	F	N/A
10	Manufacturing (shoes)	UK / Ethiopia	F	Funder & funded
11	Educational content for children in Africa	Nigeria	M	Funded
12	Fashion & lifestyle e-commerce	UK	F	Funded
13	Fine arts, arts centre co-founder & talent management	Kenya / USA	M	Funder & funded
14	Auction/fine arts	UK/Nigeria/South Africa	M	N/A

The conversations were articulated around three key themes (outlined below), which emerged from our own experience[1] with projects delivered and supported in the past. Using an interpretative approach and thematic coding of the insights provided during the conversations for the identification of sub-themes (Green and Browne, 2005), we intend to provide an understanding of the current ecosystem of CCIs financing. This chapter examines the reality faced by a range of CCIs from the perspective of various stakeholders, including investors, and explores where commonalities and gaps emerged. The conversations generated a wealth of insights for discussion beyond the subject matter of this chapter.

Understanding the finance ecosystem for CCIs in Africa

The very nature of CCIs and the associated ecosystem lies at the heart of any impactful and sustainable financing intervention. CCIs are fundamentally about the people that inhabit this ecosystem. Change thus needs to take place amongst all stakeholders; from perceptions of CCIs as a serious career to the way investors consider the CCIs and sustainably seize the opportunity. The discussion of our data is articulated around the three key themes. Firstly, the conversations provided a rich set of considerations around the current CCI financing environment. Here, resource allocation and policy paint a picture of the ecosystem in terms of what drives priority setting and allocation of funds, the opportunities and associated trends and risks. Secondly, we look to gain an understanding of the financing ecosystem from the point of view of the businesses. Although available funds and options are at the centre of the ecosystem, this section addresses the journey and experiences of the participants. Finally, we take a more detailed look at the perspectives on the support provided to businesses and how they experienced it.

An overview of the financing ecosystem for CCIs in Africa: space, data, digital and access

Space plays different roles in the financing equation. Overwhelmingly, it was presented during our conservations as an enabler for change and a key aspect in the development and financing of CCIs, requiring closer attention from investors and businesses.

For investors and providers, space supports funding allocation and the identification of promising projects and investment targets. For both businesses and investors, space also means income generation through real estate utilisation.

From the perspective of CCI businesses, although space is recognised as facilitating access to funds, skills and networks (Hauge and Hracs, 2010), there was a commonly expressed need for more empowering spaces supporting production, delivery and income generation and addressing the current lack of appropriate infrastructure (internet, electricity, supply chain), which was perceived as hampering the development and growth potential of businesses. The idea of space development is presented: "There is a need for empowering centres [...] How do you get investors into space development?" (Interviewee 1). Aspects and challenges related to available space also included availability, cost, location, access (physical as well as to information) and services provided within the space, and attitudes of users, providers and local communities and authorities.

Financing for CCIs to support growth and innovation, while addressing current gaps and avoiding duplication, requires a clear understanding of this ecosystem. This includes the nature of CCIs, perceptions, common and specific needs and gaps faced by CCIs (according to sectors and geographic location) and a clear mapping of the opportunity (financing environment and associated requirements). Though there is growing recognition of the viability of investments into CCIs across Africa, a number of challenges are yet to be addressed, including data and information, policy, the role of the digital environment, and investor approaches (see Figure 8.1).

Where there is a level of support, it was seen as hampered by difficulties with licences and permits, an opaque and fragmented network of third-party providers and brokers and the inadequacy of trade agreements and representation CCIs in existing arts councils and government bodies. Unsigned or unimplemented treaties, lack of access or difficulty in accessing international markets and funds, and a combination of a country and the industry's risk profile in the eye of investors are further barriers cited by stakeholders. The resulting effect of these external circumstances often fosters resilience amongst the creative businesses "Society fixes itself. You take it. Create attention and force consumption" (Interviewee 5).

Effective data on trade, including current and future trends and risks, is a key element in decision-making. As discussed by one of our participants "a core element to the Creative Economy is the availability of trade data on creative goods and services. Data is extremely important for governments to make informed decisions about policy" (Interviewee 9). Effective data allows for a change in the narrative of CCIs in Africa, thus impacting the spectrum for policy change, risk perception and investment flows into CCIs, as well as supporting innovation and new product and services development. Data-related drivers for the allocation of funds to CCIs cited by other respondents also include investor approaches,

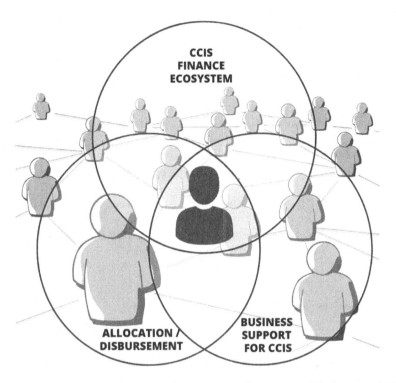

Figure 8.1 CCIs entrepreneur operating across allocation or disbursement, CCIs finance ecosystem and business support for CCIs.

which present a specific set of challenges, such as bilateral diplomacy in the case of funding by external governmental agencies and in country donor funding disbursement processes and frameworks.

In this context, data and the new digital landscape are two related aspects to be considered. Data is a commercially powerful asset; a business's database is often overlooked as UNCTAD (2018: 19) highlights "there is significant scope to activate creative economies by leveraging digital disruption and new technologies […]. Digital disruption looks set to completely re-shape trade, and the world as we know it". Demographics, employment and new income avenues enabled by the ever-evolving digital landscape give the next generation opportunities they did not previously have access to. In our research, the digital landscape was presented as an enabler of access to information, networks and online communities, education and tailored training programmes, as well as an enabler for change (online lobbying communities). It was perceived as providing entrepreneurs with not only technical insights and expertise but also with a moral boost through the sharing of common experiences and challenges. This digital landscape plays an intrinsic role in the CCIs from the way information is shared and value is created (products and processes), to offering diversification (of product/content, markets segments, channels), new avenues for revenue generation and access to funds, and to building and maintaining of new partnerships; presenting both opportunities and a whole new set of challenges for all stakeholders (UNCTAD, 2018).

There is thus a role for the private sector in galvanising change and imposing urgency on policy makers and governments:

> [technocrats] have the responsibility to tell them (policy makers) where they are getting it wrong […] we need to prove everybody wrong and be the living proof of everything that needs to change and how it can change; we need to impact policy.
>
> (Interviewee 8)

Businesses' experience in accessing finance

A common experience amongst stakeholders was the link between accessing finance and their understanding of the overall financing ecosystem. This includes the various funding and support opportunities available, and related challenges and requirements, as well as the convoluted landscape of third-party providers and brokers. Therefore, before looking to access external money, the starting point for most people interviewed was the need to be clear not only about the market, the product or service one is offering, one's own skills and knowledge gaps, the road ahead and the money required to deliver on the different phases, but also the various requirements for and conditions attached to external funding. As expressed by one of the respondents, "competition is high, and it can be hard for businesses to survive" (Interviewee 10). In her case, if her company had been a normal trading company, their risk profile would have been perceived as too high for most traditional investors.

Fundraising, including investment training and how to raise capital in a sustainable way, was the aspect most participants identified as key. It could easily become a full-time job for businesses and a distraction from the daily operations required to survive and grow. Furthermore, many participants admitted to not being well versed in fundraising and the investment landscape, unsure when they started about their capital requirements and funding processes; this is still the case for some of them. They presented their journey as one of trial and error or relying on mentors and networks for advice and access. Sometimes, this meant missing out on sources of information, support or funds that would have been available in a less opaque system. While some sought out third-party provider support, others relied on the models they were comfortable with to sustain themselves and their projects or businesses. These models are as follows:

Friends and Family remain the easiest pathway for growth money after income generation, sponsorship/corporate partnerships and self-financing.

Grants are seen as the simplest option after Friends and Family. However, the size, timing, requirements, reporting and monitoring, donor agenda, chance of success, path to growth, and lack of grants for commercial enterprises or follow-on support to be commercial were aspects often mentioned by businesses who tried this and were often reasons for which businesses chose not to go for grant money.

> [There is a] gap between donors and the private sector [...]. Donors need to take a chance and let people prove that they can accomplish [...] [we] need to radically change the old ways.
>
> (Interviewee 8)

Loans are a financing option that people are familiar with, although the cost of capital is often not attractive and puts unnecessary pressure on businesses. The number of new loan options and providers, especially in the digital age also offer more opportunities to access better suited financing options.

> Simple business loans would have been nice but the ones available there aren't conducive – loan interest rates were 20+% (so you can't do it) because you wouldn't make investors' money quickly – so it would have put too much pressure.
>
> (Interviewee 11)

When it comes to accessing money from investors, the general ecosystem of the country (including perceived risk, policies, economic situation, trade agreements, to mention but a few) was often presented as playing an important role in unlocking finance. In a number of instances, this has led those with the knowledge and skills, means and/or access to set up financing solutions or investment vehicles themselves and/or to provide businesses with the support they see as missing

Such set-ups have an important role to play in providing financing schemes and support specific for businesses in their own environments and in added-value partnerships with other stakeholders looking to enter, expand or tailor their activities in a certain country, region or sector with a strategic partner for meaningful impact. Compared to those who are setting up their own investment vehicles, many creatives now look to provide supporting platforms and environments to the next generation of creative businesses to address the gaps and challenges they faced themselves.

Collectively, this ties in with some of the innovative combinations around financing and support especially around the development of artists. These set-ups also have the potential to address the need expressed by respondents for long-term approaches by funders, including investment options with artists and tailored creative business development programmes, with applicable skills anchored in the reality of businesses.

Reflecting on the key aspects and stages of business development (see Figure 8.2), participants identified some key opportunities and challenges.

At the initial stage, they recognised the importance of having the right attitude, vision and ambition but also being focused on key markets. One of them added "focus on your market because they are the best investors you can get – get out there" (Interviewee 11). Furthermore, timing is a key aspect because gaining money too early could lead to mistakes especially in new businesses, and to investors walking away.

At this stage, the main challenges pertain to building networks and the ability to exercise resilience, patience, self-sustainability and until the business is able to scale up and be in a position to attract the right type of investments on a solid basis. This also includes the financial ability to take research and development risks, "experiment and when you feel you have a scalable product you can get investment in" (Interviewee 11) and secure the working capital for appropriate skills and infrastructure. Those who are starting out should be given the opportunity to "prove themselves and become those who have succeeded" (Interviewee 8).

At the stage where the company is building a track record and recognition, the skills and opportunities needed are slightly different. Although funds tend to be allocated to those who are already funded, even for those with international recognition and awards, if risk and investor concerns are not addressed, raising finance remains challenging. Furthermore, lack of follow-on funding for those who get early stage financing often creates a gap in which most businesses find themselves in. There is also an element of "luck and opportunity at this stage, of being at the right place at the right time; however, one needs to be agile enough to take this opportunity" (Interviewee 3).

The valuation of a business or a product and understanding how much money one needs compared to how much of the company one is

STAGE	PRE-TRADING OR PRE-SEED	SEED INVESTMENT	LAUNCH / START-UP	EARLY STAGE	MATURE COMPANY
DESCRIPTION	Idea of a business that needs to be formulated for execution	Capital needed to get the business registered and "off the ground"	Business plan, and vision detailed out. Time for product / service roll-out	Revenues are now growing, and business needs growth capital	Steady and stable business now needs balance sheet engineering for the right capital structure
INVESTORS	Angels Friends & Family Owner Capital Crowdfunding Microfinance	Angels Venture Capital Partnerships Incubators	Venture Capital PE Funds Self-Finance Grants Impact Investors Philanthropy Funds	Growth PE Funds Debt Markets Banks Debt Funds Mezzanine Funds	Secondary PE Funds Capital Markets Banks, Debt Funds Equity Injection (IPO)
RISKS	Entrepreneur Risk Idea Risk Execution Risk	Entrepreneur Risk Idea Risk Execution Risk	Management Risk Market Risk Execution Risk	Management Risk Market Risk Execution Risk Counterparty Risk Political Risk	Management Risk Market Risk Execution Risk Diversification Risk Revenue Risk Political Risk
EXPECTED ANNUAL RETURNS	30% +	25% - 30%	25%	20%	30% +

Figure 8.2 Uses and sources of funds through the traditional stages of a project/company.

prepared to give brings a specific set of challenges. In the case of artwork, valuation is needed to secure insurance, especially if leasing artwork is considered as an income stream. Valuation and insurance are still nascent and underdeveloped in a number of countries and sectors. Our research, however, shows that this aspect is very country and market specific, with some countries such as South Africa more advanced than others. In many instances, there are no straightforward determinants of the current and future value of a good or service.

Networks are a key aspect in the finance for CCIs in Africa and access is fundamental. Networks are the backbone of CCIs businesses (Potts et al., 2008), and the doors to expertise, business skills as well as to funding. One respondent equated the importance of getting partners right to that of selling them one's idea (Interviewee 10).

Though cited as a first port of call by most respondents, building and curating networks and partnerships comes with its own set of challenges. In particular, these challenges were articulated across two levels:

- Network building: finding the right networks, partners and mentors, and financing the associated time and costs.
- Managing relationships: leveraging networks and relationships requires an element of trust building (Lee, 2015). Furthermore, it involves managing people, expectations, communication, engagement, community buy-in and mistakes, which take time to rectify.

Beyond getting the right partners, participants mentioned the importance of appropriate and effective mentors as invaluable assets on an entrepreneur or business's journey. One respondent emphasised the importance of ensuring selected mentors that have the time and commitment capacity. The role of the mentee was to drive this commitment and end the relationship if the mentor was not suitable or committed (Interviewee 12).

Despite challenges, partnerships, access to information (groups) and required (peer/expert) support are improving overall. The increased number of sectoral guilds and lobbying organisations has had positive effects such as "reducing barriers to production" (Interviewee 1), facilitating access to information (especially through virtual platforms), increasing access to skills, knowledge and international partnerships, and improving access to both local and international industry and technical expertise. Furthermore, it is important to consider how practitioners are engaging in defining the space in which they operate "increasing lobbying for their own rights" (Interviewee 3). While guilds and groups bring together different categories (for example, actors, scriptwriters, filmmakers) there are still no connections between these sub-groups.

Some other people are going out there and talking to try and reverse it (the current ecosystem) but we would rather do it and make money and then come back with a case to give to them, because right now no one has had such economic potential – we need to form bodies first before government can interact with us – but we want to survive as a company first and then make our money. Once you have a case study now you can scale it up – you don't want to beg them.

(Interviewee 11)

The role of business support: what is there and what is missing

Successful business support by third parties in the context of finance for CCIs requires an understanding of the ecosystem in which the creative businesses evolve; who is out there and with what offer. Though many artists are self-taught, the literature highlights that even when coming out of higher education many struggle to think of themselves as businesses (England, 2020). The premise here was the need for "creatives to think like businesses" (Interviewee 2), knowing their offer, market and skills gaps/limitations (Interviewee 12) and to manage their expectations in order to successfully deliver on their ambitions and goals and unlock effective support and financing.

The insights provided by respondents pertaining to business support and financing were detailed and go beyond the aim of this chapter. They are summarised in Table 8.2 and will be developed in further materials. Marketing (product/service innovation and diversification) and IP and legal were aspects that interviewees felt they would need basic training on but noted that challenges were more about identifying the right providers than acquiring these skills themselves (Interviewee 7).

The most important and recurrent aspects mentioned in relation to business support were:

- Business training: turning training into opportunity and idea development and production, including investment finance/fundraising, accessing networks and valuation.
- (Self-)sustainability business models, including impact measure.
- Operational challenges: including surrounding yourself with the right teams and expertise, production and market validation (route to market) and the development of artists.

For many, an important role was and will be played by digital. In this context, digital was associated with product diversification, access to

Table 8.2 Business support for CCIs: challenges and support required.

	Challenges	Required Support
Perceptions & Informal Management of Expectations	CCIs not always seen as serious careers by peers or creatives themselves, hampering commitment and growth potential. Lack of management of expectations by creatives can hinder access to funds. Lack of balance between the creative nature of a service or product and operating like a business. Living hand to mouth and requiring support in refining business model to capitalise on lowest hanging fruits while identifying revenue streams and pathways to scale.	More visual support and tools in basic business knowledge adapted for the creative industries. Tailored skills development anchored in reality. Tailored support in identity, brand and legacy building.
Operational Challenges	Operational challenges slow down product development and delivery, especially where products are seasonal.	Operational management and industry-specific business cycles.
Idea Development & Production	Challenges to build a body of work, Minimum Viable Product (MVP) or track record, and in some instances, being first to market to unlock capital.	Translating ideas into minimum viable or feasible, scalable and exportable products, learning how to be agile and recover from mistakes, quality and capacity building, building trust from stakeholders, accessing appropriate external expertise and turning training into sustainable opportunity development.

(Continued)

Table 8.2 Continued.

	Challenges	Required Support
Market Validation	Struggle to bring a product to market, understand what the audiences and market segments want, and how to engage them. Going to market quickly without being too "precious" with one's product and letting the market drive it.	Need and opportunity assessment, route to market, supply chain and marketing outreach.
Impact Measure & Sustainable Models	Measuring impact (job creation, sustainable development goals, environment, outreach) to secure funding undeveloped.	Self-sustainability models, including non-grant dependency, and sustainable business models (including human resources, innovation and diversification).
Incubation & Acceleration	Effective value-added tailored interventions by investors and agents based on collaboration with supported businesses and a long-term view of nurturing these businesses and projects while helping them increase their sales. These interventions might include investing with, or in these businesses and projects.	Revise current workshop and incubation and acceleration models (both in physical spaces and virtual) and other business support interventions to create real added value for participants, including follow-up support and applicable skills anchored in the reality of businesses, keeping them committed and motivated.

information and networks (podcasts, communities and virtual sharing), distribution, and was positioned as an enabler for policy change (the role played by underground culture). However, as another participant highlighted

> Given the dynamic nature of creative goods and services and the sharp upturn in the pace of the digitisation of goods and services, and transactions, a core challenge is to make sure that the most dynamic parts of the Creative Economy are well captured and represented

in the statistical trade records. The solution is complex and calls for inter-agency co-operation, and nation states to innovate and operationalise measures of the digital economy. So, it will be important for all interested stakeholders to work together on the statistical area in order to find shared solutions.

(Interviewee 9)

Digital technologies were seen as requiring better tailored training programmes. In particular, monetisation, data protection and quality control were aspects felt to be lacking in training and support impeding their ability to take full advantage of the opportunities provided.

Don't think about Nigeria or local market alone, think globally [...] there are people around the world who will want to watch that content [...], don't say just Nigeria can watch [...] don't limit yourself – Nigeria might not be where you get your revenue.

(Interviewee 11)

From our experience, brokers are many but CCIs-focused business support providers are few. Across Africa, creative business support is still mainly delivered on an ad hoc basis by creatives, industry professionals and agencies. Aspects such as age, gender and sector-specific applications leave some talented people and promising projects on the sidelines. Moreover, the need for a cross-sector approach and support is still largely unaddressed. Networks of key professionals emerge from time to time (e.g. the Lagos Creative Enterprise Week) in order to meet these needs but suffer from similar unsustainable financing models as the businesses they are supporting. Incubator and accelerator partnerships are being developed in order to bridge this gap.

Conclusions and future scenarios

Despite tremendous growth and income-generation potential, there is still limited, fragmented, and – sometimes with duplication of efforts – access to finance and dedicated business advice for start-up and growth businesses in CCIs in Africa. As presented in this chapter, finance for CCIs is a broad issue encompassing a range of elements for models and policies to be sustainable, which must be anchored in and informed by both local and broader international contexts and specificities. There are key considerations underlying the design and implementation of appropriate frameworks, tools and policies to sustainably address the funding needs and gaps for CCIs in Africa. The first is the flow of capital into the creative economy; capital per se is not the issue, its deployment however is. The second is education, and the business support available to entities and projects seeking capital, required to facilitate a more mutually informed exchange between investors and recipients.

Our experience and the results presented in this chapter support the need for concerted action by all stakeholders around transparent flows of information and added-value partnerships to facilitate sustainable access by businesses to the right networks, information and data and support and expertise. These must address their pain points and allow them to reach their true potential. The momentum is there, and the opportunity is evident; we must work together to change the narrative, however. All stakeholders have a role to play in this. The narrative thus is one of movement and not inertia. A healthy and enabling medium must be found between the slower pace of institutions and policy making and the high-speed wait-for-no-green light and ask for forgiveness later approach of CCIs combined with the hunger for change of the upcoming generations.

Notes

1　HATCH provides support to individuals and organisations through the combination of consultancy, business support and access to finance. The experience and knowledge acquired through the work of HATCH contribute to the framing of the findings of this chapter.
2　We would like to acknowledge the contribution of the participants to the research project and time taken to participate and provide input into our work. We would also like to thank the editors for the feedback received.

References

DCMS (1998) *Creative Industries Mapping Document*. London, UK: Department of Culture, Media and Sport.

England L (2020) *Crafting Professionals in UK Higher Education: Craft Work Logics and Skills for Professional Practice*. London: King's College London.

Green J and Browne J (2005) *Principles of Social Research*. New York: Open University Press.

Hauge A and Hracs BJ (2010) See the sound, hear the style: Collaborative linkages between Indie musicians and fashion designers in local scenes. *Industry and Innovation* 17: 113–129.

Lee M (2015) Fostering connectivity: A social network analysis of entrepreneurs in creative industries. *International Journal of Cultural Policy* 21(2): 139–152.

Monclus RP (2015) Public banking for the cultural sector: Financial instruments and the new financial intermediaries. *International Review of Social Research* 5(2): 88–101.

Munro E (2017) Building soft skills in the creative economy: Creative intermediaries, business support and the 'soft skills gap'. *Poetics* 64: 14–25.

Potts J, Cunningham S, Hartley J et al. (2008) Social network markets: A new definition of the creative industries. *Journal of Cultural Economics* 32(3): 167–185.

Stage CW and Mattson M (2003) Ethnographic interviewing as contextualised conversation. In *Expressions of Ethnography: Novel Approaches to Qualitative Methods*. New York: SUNY Press, pp. 97–105.

UNCTAD (2018) *Creative Economy Outlook Trends in International Trade in Creative Industries Country Profiles*. Available at: https://unctad.org/en/PublicationsLibrary/ditcted2018d3_en.pdf.

UNESCO (2015) *Cultural Times the First Global Map of Cultural and Creative Industries*. Available at: https://en.unesco.org/creativity/sites/creativity/files/cultural_times._the_first_global_map_of_cultural_and_creative_industries.pdf (accessed 17/05/2020).

9 Developing the handicraft sector in South Africa

The role of policy

Oluwayemisi Adebola Abisuga-Oyekunle,
Lauren England and Roberta Comunian

Introduction

There has been growing attention from academics and policymakers on the role that the creative and cultural industries (CCIs) can play in the development of South Africa (Abisuga-Oyekunle and Sirayi, 2018; Snowball et al., 2017). Within the broader literature, the craft sector has received attention from policymakers and development agencies (UNDP and UNESCO, 2013) for its potential for job creation and international trade (UNCTAD, 2010) in contexts with poor infrastructure, including South Africa (Rhodes, 2011). Here the craft sector not only generates income for groups or individuals with access to resources but also plays an important economic role for vulnerable and/or rural communities, especially women, providing a key source of income with low access requirements (capital, resources and equipment) (Nyawo and Mubangizi, 2015; Pereira et al., 2006; Rogerson, 2000; Shackleton and Shackleton, 2004). According to a report on the South African Craft Industry (DACST, 1998: 4)

> Many rural South Africans have a low level of education and poor literacy and numeric skills [...] there are very few entry points into the economy for people to earn an income. The craft industry is one of the few entry points available to South Africans presently excluded from the formal economy.

Urbanisation and the development of tourism industries (Snowball and Courtney, 2010) are also associated with the establishment of craft economies that draw on local natural resources, artistic skills and a rich cultural heritage, particularly in the regions of Gauteng and the Western Cape (Abisuga-Oyekunle and Sirayi, 2018; DACST, 1998).

In this chapter, we specifically consider the role of policy and associated interventions in relation to crafts entrepreneurs and how this can add value to the development of their activities in rural South Africa. We investigate two main research areas and their interconnections: on one side the business motivation driving the craft entrepreneurs and the business model adopted (between making and retailing); on the other, the role that support and policy play or can play in the development of the sector.

We also argue against the international tendency to undermine the contribution of craft to the CCIs because of its informality and large number of micro enterprises which are hard to capture in data mapping exercises (Kaiser Associates, 2005). It is important that the handicraft sector and craft entrepreneurs are included in policy interventions that support the broader CCIs and are considered in their sustainable development (Oyekunle and Sirayi, 2018). Placing value on the sector as part of the national CCIs ecosystem can facilitate collaborations across a range of agents, from heritage and community organisations to marketing, digital communications and platforms able to deliver products to wider audiences and markets.

The chapter is structured in four parts. Firstly, we define handicraft and its production ecosystem, referring specifically to the South African literature and context. Here we explore business models and the role of retail in supporting the economic viability of handicraft. Secondly, we present our research methodology based on a qualitative case study in the Midlands Meander, located in the Province of KwaZulu-Natal, South Africa in 2017. We look at the data collected in the third part, focusing specifically on business motivations and orientations (in relation to the balance of production and retail) and discuss the challenges faced. We conclude by reflecting on the role of policy in the sector and the way a better knowledge of business practices and the ecosystem can help shape future developments.

Defining handicraft and its value chain

Defining handicraft

The UNESCO and International Trade Centre (ITC) report in 1997 provided one of the first definitions of the craft sector internationally:

> Products that are produced by artisans, either completely by hand or with the help of hand-tools or even mechanical means, as long as the direct manual contribution of the artisan remains the most substantial

component of the finished product [...]. The special nature of artisanal products derives from their distinctive features, which can be utilitarian, aesthetic, artistic, creative, culturally attached, decorative, functional, traditional, religiously and socially symbolic and significant.

(UNESCO and ITC, 1997: 1, Annex 2)

Within this broader definition, in general craft activities can be classified according to the materials used, namely textiles, ceramics, metal and glass, as well as natural resources such as wood, reeds, and stones, although this list is not exhaustive. Beyond classifying the materials used, crafts business can often be classified as part of other sectors, depending on the level of activities (design, fashion and visual arts) and their recognition in the market. However, we can also think about a craft value chain (Figure 9.1), in which, ideation is at the start of the process and value is added through stages of production but also through the distribution (retail and exhibition) of those artefacts and their final consumption.

In this chapter, we are specifically interested in the production and distribution stages, and their interconnected nature, in the context of small and micro craft business in South Africa, as discussed next. We argue that it is important, both from a definition and policy implementation perspective, that greater consideration is given to the connection between the making and retailing of craft products.

Handicraft value chains and the role of retail

Internationally – as well as in South Africa – there is a recognition that the craft sector mainly comprises small craft enterprises, from individual artisans and makers to small-batch handicraft producers. In South Africa specifically, these micro enterprises often have an informal setting and

CRAFT VALUE CHAIN

| 1 | 2 | 3 & 4 | 5 |
| IDEA | PRODUCTION | RETAIL & DISTRIBUTION | CONSUMERS |

Figure 9.1 A schematic representation of the craft value chain.

business structure and are connected to the livelihoods of individuals (Hay, 2008).

However, the craft sector includes a range of business, from the afore-mentioned sole traders and makers, to established exporters with the capacity to invest in marketing as well as distribution networks nationally and globally (DAC, 2016). This study invites broader considerations of the value chains (Figure 9.1) of craft in South Africa and the role that new marketing strategies and communication tools (such as websites, brochures etc.) can play in further developing the sector (DAC, 2016) and enabling South African products to reach wider audiences and markets. Evidence shows that craft producers also use various distribution channels (Makhitha, 2015, 2017); the craft artist operates in both local and international markets, selling through galleries and top retailers, while small-batch and emerging craft producers sell within their own communities through direct sales. The established and exporter enterprises have permanent premises for their business activities, while the start-up and emerging manufacturers still undertake production from home. The complexity and fragmentation of the sector makes it hard to establish a one-size-fits-all approach to marketing and business development.

In this chapter we specifically explore the context of small rural craft businesses and focus on the initial steps of the value chain, looking at what strategies are used and what support can be accessed at that level. In this context, we identify three main business categories/strategies:

(1) **The maker (production only).** This individual or small community group do not engage in opportunities to retail directly to customers but simply pass on their products to other retailers to sell. This business model often has risks regarding the inability of the maker to check the real market value or talk with potential customers for feedback.

(2) **The maker and retailer (production and retailing/distribution).** This business setting is often more demanding (in terms of human resource and potential investment in retail spaces). The maker also needs to master a range of business skills, including marketing and communication. However, it has the potential to allow the makers to interact with the market and set the price for their own (and others') work as well as receive feedback to improve or tailor production.

(3) **The retailer (marketing and distribution).** This business model is the one where more business skills are used than creative skills. Here the creative work is outsourced to (1), while the business specialises in promotion and retailing. This has potential to maximise

value creation for the individual but does require negotiation and translating customers' needs and wants down the value chain.

From the profiles outlined above, we can see the importance of retailers and intermediation skills for (2) and (3) and the way these businesses need to combine a wider range of knowledge and expertise, beyond making. According to Hay (2008), retailers are key as the market creators, able to source new products and likewise – if they build good networks and collaborative platforms with makers – they can contribute to the development of new products. However, Makhitha (2016) states that often craft producers struggle to engage with the formal market via specialised retailers, and resort to selling directly to consumers either at the flea market or factory floor. While this gives them an awareness of their consumers, it does not necessarily feedback into their production and R&D. For rural craft producers this can be further limited by their locality away from popular markets (Periera et al., 2006), although potential to tap into local tourist markets (i.e. nearby nature reserves) has been identified (ibid.). Formal market access is also hindered by the presence of imported products in local markets, which creates further challenges for small producers (Makhitha, 2017). Further issues in conflict with economic development and poverty alleviation efforts focused on craft include socio-economic and ethnic divisions in formal market access; Makhitha (2016) discusses the way craft retail channels are connected to specific markets segments, which are also segmented in relation to the ethnic origin of producers; mainstream craft retail activities (i.e. craft markets and galleries) are used by White craft producers, while "craft producers owned by Blacks and coloured people are mainly sold through informal markets due to limited access to capital, resources and technology" (Makhitha, 2016: 669).

Data and policy context in South Africa

Current data and knowledge on Craft in South Africa

The most recent statistical overview of the craft sector is provided by the South Africa Cultural Observatory (SACO, 2019). Amongst their rich data, there are some interesting characteristics discussed. Firstly, the Visual Arts and Craft (VAC) domain in their research is one of the most diverse cultural occupations, with 82.4% of workers being Black African, 10.9% coloured people, and 1.2% of Indian/Asian origin and only 5.6% being White. However, in this domain there is a "lower proportion of young people (30%), but a higher proportion of middle-aged (35 – 49 years old) workers (44.4% in the VAC domain, compared to 38.7% in cultural workers overall)" (SACO, 2019: 17). Furthermore, older women are more heavily involved in the sector than young women.

Other characteristics of the sector are presented by Nyawo and Mubangizi's (2015) study of the KwaZulu-Natal region. They suggest that the craft sector is perceived to be the domain of women, although there are disciplinary divides – men dominate sub-sectors such as wood-carving, metalwork and painting. They also highlight that 90% of crafters only have very low levels of education and that for 60% of their house-holds there are no other forms of employment or income beyond the one derived by craft (ibid.).

The role of policy in craft development

As discussed, policy plays an important role in defining but also shaping the current and future dynamics of the sector.

The SACO (2019) report on the state of the VAC sector provides an extensive review of the South African policy interventions in these areas under the following headlines:

> Developing of interdepartmental collaboration; improving market access for the craft; improving infrastructure; providing education, training and technical skills; encouraging small and micro business and entrepreneurships in the crafts sector; providing access to fund-ing for the crafts sector; linking tourism to the VAC domain; where practical, to enforce intellectual property rights, and to encourage ongoing design innovation to maintain competitiveness.
>
> (SACO, 2019: 12)

Reviewing this existing literature and building on SACO's (2019) work, in Figure 9.2 we summarise the interconnections of craft with multiple – sometimes overlapping – policy agendas in South Africa, although this could be applied to many other national contexts. These can be grouped under four headings, although many considerations connect across policy fields:

Craft and Economic Policy: craft is seen as an opportunity for poverty alle-viation and Nyawo and Mubangizi (2015) specifically consider its relationship with tourism (and its spillover effects). The opportunity to start-up small businesses, potentially with a low initial investment, is seen as a means of promoting entrepreneurship across a range of social groups, often from a less fortunate economic background.

Figure 9.2 Connecting craft and policy agendas.

Craft and Education Policy: craft also connects with education policy. In particular, the opportunity to provide specific craft skills and upskill part of the population is critical to strengthen policies for inclusion (in social and economic policies). Furthermore, as discussed in the first four chapters of this book, the opportunity to expand creative education in Africa can respond to the interest of its growing youth.

Craft and Social Policy: craft is also seen as an essential tool to respond to youth unemployment, connecting with the economic and education agendas discussed above in relation to wealth and job creation (Abisuga-Oyekunle and Fillis, 2017). The gender and diversity agenda is also very important as craft, as discussed above, has been considered particularly accessible to often marginalised groups in society.

Craft and Cultural Policy: craft is seen as an essential means through which cultural heritage and traditions are reproduced but also reinvented and renewed over time. As making traditions have a close association with local materials and community practices, this can add value by connecting with opportunities for cultural participation and bottom-up engagement in inclusive and participatory forms.

Research methodology, sample and data

The data presented in this chapter are the results of a funded[1] project undertaken in the Midlands Meander, located in the Province of KwaZulu-Natal, South Africa during June and July 2017. Qualitative data collection was conducted using in-depth interviews with 21 individuals involved in craft businesses in the area. Midlands Meander has an attractive arts and craft route that attracts local and international tourists with specific interests in handicrafts (Magi and Nzama, 2009; McCarthy and Mavundla, 2009). Interviews were recorded, and tallying, coding, text analysis and content analysis of transcripts were undertaken when performing qualitative data analysis (Ritchie et al., 2013). The respondents were selected to represent three types of craft businesses: craft makers (only); craft makers and retailers; craft retailers (only).

Table 9.1 presents demographic and business characteristics of our respondents. Eleven of the interviewees were male and ten were female. There was no clear distinction between males and females regarding the type of craft they made or sold. About 12 different categories of craft are being produced and retailed by the respondents, from beads to wooden masks, from drums to lace. This is representative of the diversity and variety of South Africans' craft production (Kaiser Associates, 2005). Regarding the type of enterprise activities, seven interviewees were makers and retailers (M&R) of craft products, seven were makers only (M) and seven were retailers only (R).

Most of the interviewees (76%, n = 16) stated they had no prior artisan training in craft business, although they did not discuss how they acquired knowledge and experience in the production of craft products. Three M&R interviewees stated they had previous artisan training (six months of carpentry, two weeks of sales training and six months of sewing) while only one maker (six months fine and visual arts training) and one retailer (one-week bead making) had artisan training. This corresponds with the literature, which notes low levels of formal training amongst craft producers, with self-teaching and community-based learning being common (Makhitha, 2017; Nyawo and Mubangizi, 2015).

Out of the total number of interviewees, 15 were Black, while there were three Indians and three Whites, respectively. Table 9.1 shows that 8 (38%) of the interviewees are in the age group (41–50), 8 (33%) are aged

Table 9.1 Interviewees' profiles, classified as M&R (maker and retailers), M (makers) and R (retailers).

Number & Classification	Gender	Age	Ethnicity	Education	Type of Craft	Experience (Years)
#1M&R	Male	41–50	Black	Grade 12	Wooden masks, sculptures and hat knitting	14
#2M&R	Male	31–40	Black	Grade 11	Grass picnic baskets, grass sun hats, grass mats	9
#3M&R	Female	21–30	Black	Post-graduate	Traditional attires, beads	10
#4M&R	Male	41–50	Black	Grade 12	Wooden drums, side tables animal skin shields	10
#5M&R	Female	41–50	Black	Primary school	Beaded shoes, plastic plate mats, beaded necklaces	20
#6M&R	Female	21–30	Black	Post-graduate	Beads, traditional attires	10
#7M&R	Female	31–40	Indian	Post-graduate	Beads, cow skin carpets	5
#8M	Female	21–30	White	Grade 12	Knitting, tapestry, embroidery	7
#9M	Male	21–30	Black	Grade 12	Decorated clay pots	6
#10M	Male	21–30	Black	Grade 12	Flower container with beads, wire bowls, wire baskets	10
#11M	Female	41–50	Black	Grade 12	Lace, beaded necklace, beaded shoes	35
#12M	Male	21–30	Black	Grade 11	Painting, coffee drawing (painting), print making (wood cut)	4

(Continued)

Table 9.1 Continued.

Number & Classification	Gender	Age	Ethnicity	Education	Type of Craft	Experience (Years)
#13M	Female	31–40	Black	Grade 12	Traditional shoes	1
#14M	Male	41–50	Black	Grade 11	Shield and spear, clay bowls, wooden spoons	11
#15R	Female	21–30	Black	Grade 12	Grass bowls, sculptured people image	3
#16R	Female	41–50	Black	Grade 12	Woven blankets, carved wood sculptures	10
#17R	Female	41–50	Indian	Primary school	Bead works, ceramics, sculptures	30
#18R	Male	41–50	Black	Degree	Beaded shoes, neck wear, calabash drum	5
#19R	Male	31–40	Indian	Grade 12	Beaded shoes, Beaded bags	4
#20R	Male	21–30	White	Grade 12	Wooden photo frames	6
#21R	Male	51–60	White	Grade 12	Wooden chairs, wooden coffee table	3

(31–40), while 4 (19%) are in the (21–30) group, and only 2 (10%) are in the age group (51–60). None of the respondents were below age 21.

Understanding craft business in South Africa: motivation, business models and challenges

Motivations for Craft Business

The interviewees were asked why they were pursuing a craft and Table 9.2 presents a number of economic (i.e. earning an income) and non-economic reasons (i.e. supporting youth engagement in traditional craft or keeping busy in retirement) given for engaging in their type of small craft enterprise.

Economic motivations were highest amongst all groups (38% earn an income and 29% support my family), although some interviewees stated multiple economic motivations (to earn an income and support their family), while others combined economic and non-economic motivations (to earn an income and for the love of craft work). As highlighted by this respondent:

> This is like a family business because I learnt the trade from my grandmother. My other uncle is also in the business. Also, two of my other siblings have their own craft shop, although, we trade in different crafts. I am addicted to making craft and love what I am doing. [...] The handicraft business is good and helped me to earn income without much stress.
>
> (#8M, White, Female)

Table 9.2 Motivation for craft business.

Reason Given	Number of Interviewees	Percentage of Interviewees
Earn an Income	8	38
Support my Family	6	29
Family Business	1	5
Love of Craft/Craft Work	3	14
Encourage Youth Participation	2	9.5
Preserve Tradition/Heritage	2	9.5
Status/Recognition for Craft Skill and Creativity	2	9.5
Hobby/Keeping Busy	2	9.5

A love of craft or craft work (14%) was however only mentioned by makers (n = 2) or makers/retailers (n = 1), as highlighted by one maker here:

> I have worked as a permanent employee before but quit after working for 15 years. I love creativity and creating my one design, so I decided to go into handicraft production. [...] I want to be recognised in the future as a great crafter. The business is very lucrative and can build an African culture and tourism.
>
> (#13M, Female, Black)

Makers and retailers primarily had economic motivations (income, support for family or continuing a family business) or saw the craft business as a means of keeping busy, although one also aimed to encourage youth participation in craft. There is a strong connection with the opportunity for craft to be combined with other business activities, as outlined by one of the craft retailers:

> My passion for handicraft made me go into the trade. I just started the business 3 years ago and have never regretted being in the trade. I have a hotel with full engagement of tourism activities in Midland and Durban, but not much infrastructure to attract tourist. I see handicraft as tourist products and also have a shop in my hotel for sales and display of African craft works. The craft business cannot sustain itself or even me, but the income is good to support other business.
>
> (#21R, Male, White)

These findings, while based on a small number of examples, serve to highlight the varied motivations for pursuing craft business in South Africa. In order to support this diversity, a range of supporting infrastructure, markets and policies are required.

Craft business activity and revenues

While only 21 interviewees were in the sample and therefore no statistical significance can be established, it is important to compare the status, and sales performance of the interviewees.

To present this, interviewees were categorised according to their business status as either involved in making, retailing and making and retailing (see Table 9.1) based on the performance of their monthly enterprise activities. The limit level of R10,000 is based on average gross household incomes in South Africa (Statistics South Africa, 2017). For the purpose of this study, interviewees with a monthly gross household income of less than R9,990 (approximately R120,000 per year) are considered "poor" or "low income".

As illustrated in Figure 9.3, interviewees' monthly income varied substantially; 76% (n = 16) of respondents reported a low monthly sales performance of below R10,000, while 24% (n = 5) experienced a high monthly sales performance of above R10,000. Only two (9.5%) interviewees received the highest amount of R24,000 monthly from craft sales. Figure 9.3 indicates that the lowest sales obtained amongst all interviewees were by those engaged in craft production (maker/retailer and maker only). In particular, none of the 'makers' obtained a monthly gross income above the average gross household income of R10,000 and this category has the lowest average monthly sales (R7,429). This indicates that the craft makers do not earn a sustainable amount of income from their products. In contrast, those involved as retailers obtained the highest monthly sales; three out of the seven retail only interviewees experienced gross monthly earnings above R12,000, with the highest being R24,000.

There are many factors that contribute to how much can be earned monthly from craft products – Makhado and Kepe (2006) identify factors such as the demand of household duties; infrastructure (i.e. electricity); the amount of time the producer is able to invest in the process of craft; the amount of money customers are inclined to pay for an item; the quality of the product and the effort put into selling the product. Kaiser Associates (2005) also state that the majority of craft producers are small enterprises operating in an informal economy. These factors all have implications for how craft producers can sustain their livelihood or make decisions on the future sustainability of their business. As the SACO report (2019: 5) notes, "a challenge for 'survivalist' crafters is that they may become trapped in a vicious cycle, where margins are too low to allow reinvestment".

Interviewees acknowledged the challenge of inconsistent income (#5M&R) and identified a number of strategies including having a permanent job and means from family business (#8M), pursuing additional non-craft activity (#19R) and getting involved in other tourism activities (#12M) which could enable them to earn more (#13M).

> I operate other businesses apart from selling of crafts. [...] I entered the craft market because I love African tradition. I am also a businessman and cannot rely on just one business. [...] Sales of crafts alone cannot sustain me and family, but through it I was able to create employment for my two staff working in the shop.
>
> (#19R, Male, Indian)

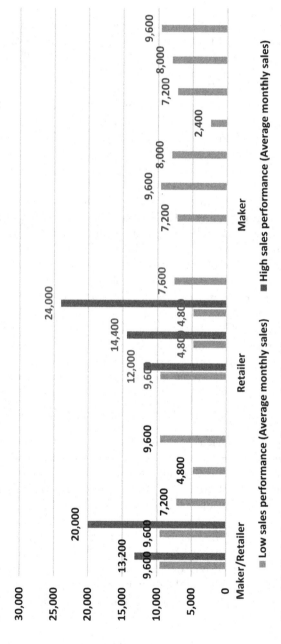

Figure 9.3 The business status, and performance levels of the interviewees.

The income earned from craft is not consistent. Some people dropped out of the business when there is not enough capital to do the business. For instance, my sister left the craft production when the competition with china products makes the demand for traditional crafts dropped.

(#5M&R, Female, Black)

Forms of support for craft business

We discussed with the craft businesses what forms of support were accessed. In general, as summarised in Table 9.3, most did not access any form of support (16 out of 21 businesses). However, for the minority who were able to access support, this was spread between different aspects of the business. Technical skills and production space was meaningful for makers, while access to materials and equipment was used by makers and retailers, potentially suggesting a 'scaling-up' of activities. Retailers seem to be accessing or interested in accessing more training – which might be connected with business development training.

The interviewees did not have great expectations of the role that policy should play. In fact, in many cases they perceived support as being about their family or networks connections. For example, one interviewee mentioned the role of her husband in encouraging and providing capital for her business (#13M), while another mentioned the lack of parental support to finish his studies.

I dropped out of high school at grade 11 due to lack of funding from my father. I got a job as an office clerk and could save money to pay for my training programme to learn decorative arts (painting and sculpture). [...]. I was able to earn a considerable income that could sustain me and family and train my siblings.

(#12M, Male, Black)

Table 9.3 Access to support.

Form of Support	Makers	Makers & Retailers	Retailers
Equipment/Tools	0	1	0
Raw Materials	0	3	0
Technical Skills	2	0	1
Production Space	1	0	0
Other Training	0	0	2
None	4	4	4

For others, the need for capital and the inability to access a loan remained a barrier to future development. "I need capital to help my business, but I do not know how, because I have approached my bank and could not get a loan [...] I have no skill, money, and training" (#16, Female, Black).

Two interviewees (#7, #20) mentioned they received support from an NGO and the bank respectively, and one (#10) had applied for funding but was awaiting feedback.

> I have received a support from an NGO for raw materials before but have not been able to receive any from the government or its agencies. I have approached some government agencies, for example, the Department of Trade and Industry (DTI) for funding to support my business in the last two years ago, but no success yet.
>
> (#7M&R, Female, Indian)

> I applied for a support at the National Empowerment Fund (NEF) for funding to buy an equipment to assist my production process, but it is not yet approved. I waste too much time with producing manually and local customers will only want to pay little, this have made the business very difficult. If the government can assist with money for machines this will compliment making with hand tools. There is also need for a good facility and space for production, I make the product from this very small space, which is not helping my business.
>
> (#10, Male, Black)

The business owners were eloquent about the need for support and the role that craft can play, not merely in their livelihoods but within the broader agendas of policy.

> I started this business when I could not get a job after school and learned the production from my employees. The handicraft business is like any other industry, and it is more important than any other business because this is African heritage, I am proud of the business, but it needs capital and skill training to grow.
>
> (#7MR, Female, Indian)

In general, beyond funding, the value of skills and training was acknowledged in relation to the opportunity to bring the sector together, strategically.

> The committee of this tourist route have organised workshops for us before through the Small Enterprise Finance Agency (SEFA) and

the Department of Arts and Culture (DAC). A lot of crafters did not attend, so they stopped coming, at least for some time now, something like workshop or training could have let our voice be heard. Through a workshop attended I was able to get a loan from the bank to support my business, and this has really helped a lot to buy wholesale and import craft items from other Africa countries.

(#20R, Male, White)

Conclusions

The chapter builds on existing knowledge of the craft sector in South Africa before exploring some of the current knowledge in connection with the rural context of Midlands Meander in more detail. In this case study, the work and practices of 21 craft businesses are described and discussed. In particular, we highlight how motivations and business earnings can vary significantly. Furthermore, the option and opportunities to be involved in retail activities (as a maker and retailer or retailer only) can make a significant difference in the financial stability of the businesses, but also in their potential knowledge and skills. In exploring the motivations, workings and business practices of these craft businesses, we also reflect on the role policy can play. We begin theoretically, but then explore this in practice through the lens of the craft businesses studied. Even in our small sample, it was clear that support was considered highly valuable not only for personal economic advancement but also for the growth of craft, heritage and local communities. While access to business funding was often limited and not widely available, the form of support mentioned most was skills and training. This also connects with opportunities for makers to potentially expand into retailing, which – from our data – seems to provide a more sustainable livelihood. Finally, and most importantly, skills and training did not just connect with the economic and social development agenda but also with cultural and educational aims in relation to cultural development and participation; it offered opportunities to support the creative aspirations of individuals involved in the sector more closely. As one of the respondents stated, "I have applied to enrol for school training in craft, because I want to be the best craft producer in KwaZulu-Natal" (#13M, Female, Black). Ultimately, the role of policy in craft is to make sure that everyone can have such aspirations.

Note

1 The authors would like to acknowledge the support of the South African National Research Fund (NRF)/Department of Science and Technology, South African Research Chair (SARChI) Initiative for funding for this project.

References

Abisuga-Oyekunle OA and Fillis IR (2017) The role of handicraft micro-enterprises as a catalyst for youth employment. *Creative Industries Journal* 10(1): 59–74.

Abisuga Oyekunle OA and Sirayi M (2018) The role of creative industries as a driver for a sustainable economy: A case of South Africa. *Creative Industries Journal* 11(3): 225–244.

DAC (2016) *Exploring New Markets: A Guide to Export for Craft Producers, Designers and Other Creatives.* Available at: http://www.dac.gov.za/sites/default/files/Explorin g-New-Markets.pdf (accessed 11/06/2020).

DACST (1998) *Cultural Industries Growth Strategy (CIGS) the South African Craft Industry Report.* Available at: https://www.gov.za/sites/default/files/gcis_docume nt/201409/cigs0.pdf (accessed 15/06/2020).

Hay D (2008) *The Business of Craft and Crafting the Business.* Pietermaritzburg: University of KwaZulu-Natal.

Kaiser Associates (2005) *Craft First Paper: The Scope of the Craft Industry in the Western Cape.* Available at: https://www.westerncape.gov.za/other/2005/11/final_firs t_paper_craft.pdf (accessed 15/06/2020).

Magi L and Nzama TA (2009) Tourism strategies and local community responses around the World Heritage Sites in KwaZulu-Natal. *South African Geographical Journal* 91(2): 94–102.

Makhado Z and Kepe T (2006) Crafting a livelihood: local-level trade in mats and baskets in Pondoland, South Africa. *Development Southern Africa* 23(4): 497–509.

Makhitha K (2015) Supply chain practices and challenges in the craft industry in Gauteng, South Africa. *Journal of Applied Business Research* 31(6): 2197–2212.

Makhitha K (2016) Marketing strategies of small craft producers in South Africa: Practices and challenges. *Journal of Applied Business Research (JABR)* 32(3): 663–680.

Makhitha K (2017) Challenges affecting small craft producer business growth and survival in South Africa. *Journal of Business and Retail Management Research* 11(3): 1–12.

McCarthy A and Mavundla K (2009) Craft as an economic enterprise: Strategies for alternative livelihoods in Kwazulu-Natal. *Small Enterprise Development Agency* 5(1): 34–42.

Nyawo J and Mubangizi BC (2015) Art and craft in local economic development: Tourism possibilities in Mtubatuba local municipality. *African Journal of Hospitality, Tourism and Leisure* 4(2): 1–15.

Oyekunle OA and Sirayi M (2018) The role of design in sustainable development of handicraft industries. *African Journal of Science, Technology, Innovation and Development* 10(4): 381–388.

Pereira T, Shackleton C and Shackleton S (2006) Trade in reedbased craft products in rural villages in the Eastern Cape, South Africa *Development Southern Africa,* 23(4): 477–495.

Rhodes S (2011) Beyond 'nourishing the soul of a nation': Craft in the context of South Africa. In *Making Futures: The Crafts as Change Maker in Sustainably Aware Cultures,* p. 2.

Ritchie J, Lewis J, Nicholls CM, et al. (2013) *Qualitative Research Practice: A Guide for Social Science Students and Researchers*. London: Sage.

Rogerson C (2000) Rural handicraft production in the developing world: policy isues for South Africa. *Agrekon* 39: 193–217.

SACO (2019) *Unpacking the Disparity Between Employment Levels and Contribution to GDP Within the Craft Sector*. Available at: https://www.southafricanculturalobs ervatory.org.za/article/unpacking-the-disparity-between-employment-levels-a nd-contribution-to-gdp-within-the-craft-sector (accessed 12/06/2020).

Shackleton C and Shackleton S (2004) The importance of non-timber forest products in rural livelihood security and as safety nets: a review of evidence from South Africa. *South African Journal of Science* 100: 658–64.

Snowball J, Collins A and Tarentaal D (2017) Transformation and job creation in the cultural and creative industries in South Africa. *Cultural Trends* 26(4): 295–309.

Snowball JD and Courtney S (2010) Cultural heritage routes in South Africa: Effective tools for heritage conservation and local economic development? *Development Southern Africa* 27(4): 563–576.

Statistcs South Africa (2017) *General Household Survey*. Available at: http://www.stat ssa.gov.za/publications/P0318/P03182017.pdf.

UNCTAD (2010) *Creative Economy Report 2010: Creative economy - A feasible development option*. Geneva: UNCTAD.

UNDP and UNESCO (2013) Creative economy report: Widening local development pathways. In *Report Prepared by Isar Y (ed)*. Paris: UNDP/UNESCO.

UNESCO and ITC (1997) *Final Report of the International Symposium on Crafts and the International Market: Trade and Customs Codification*. Available at: http://uis.unes co.org/en/glossary-term/craft-or-artisanal-products (accessed 09/06/2020).

10 Conclusions

Roberta Comunian, Brian J. Hracs and Lauren England

The book has brought together a range of perspectives and reflections on the role played by higher education (HE) and policy for the development of creative economies in Africa. We would like to conclude the book by teasing out some broader themes and presenting some recommendations for the development of creative economies in Africa based on the contributions and our research project.[1] Our considerations focus on three areas: the role of HE for the development of creative economies in Africa; the importance of understanding policy for creative economies in Africa within historical and systematic perspectives; and finally, the importance of HE as a creative intermediary which connects creative economies and policy. We also provide three policy reflections which we hope will be useful to HE leaders and policymakers working in this field.

Role of HE in the development of creative economies in Africa

The first four chapters of the book have given us supporting evidence to argue for the importance of the development of skills and education opportunities regarding the creative economies in Africa. Skills and education are certainly in demand because of the growing demand of African youth who want to engage in the creative and cultural industries (CCIs) and their opportunities (Ruyembe, 2014). However, more broadly they have the capacity to give the creative economy a voice internationally and to compete – not only economically – with other content creators worldwide, as argued by Comunian and Kimera (Chapter 5). In the sectors discussed in the various chapters – from the arts and fashion to film and theatre studies – education is allowing students and practitioners to learn from each other and contribute to the broader knowledge and expertise within the sector. HE, with its research and development practices, can also move the perspective of Africa's creative economy from being based on heritage and the richness of traditions to one that supports the need for creativity to be fostered and honed towards achieving inter-nationally recognised quality and excellence. In this framework, HE plays a specific and unique role but only if it can engage with local, national and international creative economies. From the research presented in the first four chapters and our experience, it is clear that there are opportuni-ties and advantages in a more robust framework of collaboration between HE and the local practitioners, industries or associations that shape the creative economies in each city or town. However, there are also many barriers; the book identifies three main issues in particular. Firstly, the lack of formal frameworks and transparent incentives to support col-laborations. When they do take place, they are often happening despite bureaucratic walls, as discussed by Obia et al. (Chapter 2) and by Bello (Chapter 3), based on individuals' goodwill, rather than in acknowledge-ment of their value. Secondly, the under-recognition of the CCIs as an essential economic, cultural and development partner for HE. The lack of attention towards CCIs is highlighted by Obia et al. (Chapter 2) but also by England et al. (Chapter 4) in the case of fashion in Kenya. It can be also demonstrated in the context of the African Research Universities Alliance (ARUA). The organisation has supported the establishment of more than 13 centres for excellence and research collaborations across 16 leading African research universities on a range of key development themes. However, none of the activities engages with cultural develop-ment and the creative economy.[2] While other international bodies, such as UNESCO, are lobbying and promoting the creative economies as being an essential element of inclusive and sustainable development, the HE sector must engage more fully with this research and policy agenda. Finally, it is easy to observe a common practice of many young crea-tives choosing to 'study abroad' as a pathway into the creative economy. While this is valuable for the individual and can introduce innovative and diverse ideas into the local creative ecosystem, it often exacerbates a system of inequality where it is not the most talented or deserving who emerge, but merely those who can afford specific opportunities and advantages. This has the potential to create and reinforce patterns of inequality in creative careers (Booyens, 2012). This, of course, connects with broader arguments of access and equality in HE. However, crea-tive disciplines must provide opportunities for a diverse range of young people to add to their diversity and creativity.

Understanding policy for creative economies in Africa within a historical and systematic perspective

The reflections of Oni et al. (Chapter 6), as well as Drummond and Drummond (Chapter 7) reveal the importance of looking at cultural policy development over time. They specifically highlight how policy interventions – even long before the creative economies became a popular feature of international discourses (UNDP and UNESCO, 2013) – have shaped the development trajectories of the creative economies in many African countries. Further research is needed to provide more in-depth analysis and reflection on these historical patterns and previous trajectories. It is easy to limit our understanding to the global reach of policy discourses – such as creative cities/clusters or creative economy – from the Global North to the Global South. Sternberg (2017) highlights that their reach and success is connected to the fact that they often require low infrastructural investments, but also that they are associated with a 'feel good factor' – such as promoting local cultures – which tends to receive broader political support. On the contrary, the complexity of definitions and historical accounts of how each nation or region has approached creative economies development is crucial to our contemporary understanding. It has a bearing on how creative economies are defined and articulated locally, as well as how policy has provided (or ignored in some cases) the support needed by the sector. Another critical dimension, addressed by Mokuolu et al. (Chapter 8) and Adebola-Oyekunle et al. (Chapter 9), is the importance of looking at policy for creative economies in Africa systemically. This allows for considerations to emerge in two different directions. Firstly, looking at top-down policy initiatives. While cultural policy is often overlooked and under-financed in both national and local contexts, other policy areas such as youth participation or poverty alleviation, might provide platforms and initiatives where creative economies can lead and shape new discourses of inclusive and sustainable development (Wilson et al., 2020). Concomitantly, bottom-up perspectives, as in the case of creative intermediaries aiming to expand or facilitate collaboration for financing CCIs or entrepreneurs trying to access finance – discussed by Mokuolu et al. (Chapter 8) – can give CCIs and intermediaries a coordinating role. This can empower them to create connections across different stakeholders and policymakers and to define an essential area of work and shape it to facilitate the development of creative economies.

HE as intermediary operating across creative economies, youth, policy and local development

A red thread in our research network project and this book is the emergence of HE not merely as a player in the creative economies and their local and national ecosystem, but also as a valuable intermediary engaging with a range of stakeholders and concerns (Comunian and Gilmore, 2016). Furthermore, HE seems to have the potential to play a coordinating and facilitating role, connecting national and local stakeholders.

In particular, as highlighted in Figure 10.1, we have discussed the role of HE in supporting creative economies. However, here we also notice how HE can demonstrate and argue for the value of creative economies across a range of policy initiatives from economic development to community engagement. They can do this via research expertise and international networks. The example of the South African Cultural Observatory (SACO)[3] bridging academic research with the national cultural policy can be seen as a world-leading example of these forms of collaboration. HE can play a role in translating – sometimes complex – policy frameworks to practitioners and it can distil broader – sometimes abstract – developmental goals into actions connected to local cultural and economic development. Examples include the University of Lagos with its Entrepreneurship and Skill Development Centre or the Lagoon Gallery started by the Department of Creative Arts. The importance of the HE sector in supporting the development of creative hubs is well

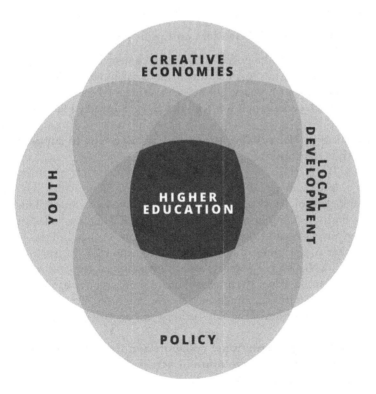

Figure 10.1 Higher education as an intermediary across creative economies, youth, policy and local development.

documented (Ashton and Comunian, 2019) and African HE is already acknowledging the value they can bring in these creative networks. The connection between HE and local development is well researched internationally. However, there has been a call for a more grounded and genuine engagement of African HE in the production of knowledge that is valued and applicable in their local contexts rather than imported from the Global North (Okolie, 2003). In our fieldwork, we observed instances of distrust or detachment between creative economies practitioners and policy both concerning economic and cultural development. However, HE institutions and their workforce are recognised as an essential player able to translate or engage with some industry needs while connecting with young people who aspire to enter the CCIs or to shape their future work. Therefore, HE also plays a vital role in youth development across Africa (Chimanikire, 2009) and in connecting youth with both the creative economies and policy agendas related to inclusion, employment and development.

Policy reflections for HE leaders and policymakers

These reflections aim to be possible policy directions which HE leaders and policymakers can use to think about the development of creative economies in Africa. Of course, some of them might be more or less applicable in each context, but we hope they remain broadly relevant.

(1) Investing in HE collaborations and partnerships to support creative economies

There is a need to invest in HE, specifically towards subjects that represent a pipeline of talent and expertise for creative economies. This concerns both creative occupations but also essential support roles to develop creative economies infrastructure such as law, finance and retailing. Whether in the context of emerging international hubs, such as Nollywood in Nigeria, or contexts where international recognition is lacking, HE can add value. It can contribute to the sector's research and development and its human capital and therefore maximise the impact of the local creative economies on their national and international profiles.

(2) Strengthening international collaboration for creative economies research and development across Africa

The network we developed across Africa through the research project has highlighted the value that African HE researchers place on international collaborations and connections. The knowledge we brought and shared was always welcomed but also re-framed and contextualised within the local infrastructure and practices. More of these research networks should be developed to support African HE in engaging with creative economies and beyond. While we shared our previous knowledge, the most critical elements of innovation and cross-fertilisations came from the interaction of participants from different African countries. We hope that research organisations like ARUA and existing exchange programmes across Africa take creative economies on board as an important agenda for the whole sector.

(3) **Making sure HE opportunities are open to many, representing the diversity of each nation or region**

While it is easy to promote the positive contribution of HE to creative economies, it is also important to consider emerging power dimensions (Comunian, 2017). HE, in many countries globally, already risks being exclusionary, leaving behind part of local youth from educational attainment and the less formalised or emerging components of creative economies from partnerships or collaborations. It is critical, in consideration of the multi-cultural nature of many African countries and regions, that opportunities are shared across cultural boundaries to allow their cultural diversity to become a resource for development and to connect with inclusivity and sustainability as the essence of creative economies (Wilson et al., 2020).

Notes

1 Arts and Humanities Research Council (grant number AH/P005950/1).
2 A full list of the ARUA centres of excellence is available at https://arua.org.za/coe./
3 The South African Cultural Observatory (SACO) was initiated by the Department of Arts and Culture in 2011. It is now hosted by Nelson Mandela University, in partnership with Rhodes University, University of KwaZulu-Natal and the University of Fort Hare, but operates nationally. For more information seeht tps://www.southafricanculturalobservatory.org.za.

References

Ashton D and Comunian R (2019) Universities as creative hubs: Modes and practices in the UK context. In: Gill R, Pratt AC and Tarek E (eds) *Creative Hubs in Question*. Cham: Palgrave Macmillan, pp. 359–379.
Booyens I (2012) Creative industries, inequality and social development: Developments, impacts and challenges in Cape Town. *Urban Forum* 23: 43–60.

Chimanikire DP (2009) *Youth and Higher Education in Africa. The Cases of Cameroon, South Africa, Eritrea and Zimbabwe: The Cases of Cameroon, South Africa, Eritrea, and Zimbabwe.* Oxford: African Books Collective.

Comunian R (2017) Creative collaborations: The role of networks, power and policy. In: Shiach M and Virani T (eds) *Cultural Policy, Innovation and the Creative Economy.* London: Palgrave Springer, pp. 231–244.

Comunian R and Gilmore A (2016) *Higher Education and the Creative Economy: Beyond the Campus.* Abingdon: Routledge.

Okolie AC (2003) Producing knowledge for sustainable development in Africa: Implications for higher education. *Higher Education* 46(2): 235–260.

Ruyembe C (2014) Sustainable creative career development pathways for young people in Tanzania: A case study. *International Journal of Social Sciences and Entrepreneurship* 1(9): 366–377.

Sternberg R (2017) Creativity support policies as a means of development policy for the global South? A critical appraisal of the UNESCO creative economy report 2013. *Regional Studies* 51(2): 336–345.

UNDP and UNESCO (2013) Creative economy report: Widening local development pathways. In: *Report Prepared by Isar Y (ed).* Paris: UNDP/UNESCO.

Wilson N, Gross J, Dent T, et al. (2020) *Re-thinking Inclusive and Sustainable Growth for the Creative Economy: A Literature Review.* Available at: https://disce.eu/wp-content/uploads/2020/01/DISCE-Report-D5.2.pdf (accessed 17/04/2020).

Index

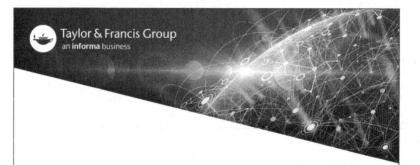

Printed in the United States
by Baker & Taylor Publisher Services